SPEED BUMPS

A Student-Friendly Guide to Qualitative Research

SPEED BUMPS

A Student-Friendly Guide to Qualitative Research

Lois Weis
Michelle Fine

TEACHERS COLLEGE PRESS

Teachers College, Columbia University
New York and London

Published by Teachers College Press, 1234 Amsterdam Avenue, New York, NY 10027

Library of Congress Cataloging-in-Publication Data

Speed Bumps : a student-friendly guide to qualitative research / Lois Weis and Michelle Fine.
    p. cm.
  Includes bibliographical references and index.
  ISBN 0-8077-3966-9 (pbk.)
  1. Social sciences—Research. 2. Qualitative research. I. Weis, Lois. II. Fine, Michelle.
  H62 .S72966 2000
  001.4'2—dc 21   00-024445

ISBN 0-8077-3966-9 (paper)

Printed on acid-free paper

Manufactured in the United States of America

07 06 05 04 03 02 01 00   8 7 6 5 4 3 2 1

CONTENTS

ACKNOWLEDGMENTS

This collection represents the intellectual, political, and manual labor of so many. We thank broadly the students, educators, activists, and the communities with which we have worked, and we thank specifically Adrianne Christmas, Amy Ferry, Steven Fine, Jenni Hoffman, Susan Ott, and Susan Weseen for their ceaseless dedication to producing this volume in a very short time. Carole Saltz and Susan Liddicoat provided support and technical assistance, without which we would simply have no volume.

Speed Bumps is dedicated to new researchers, eager to engage, cautious about the work, and committed to a practice of ethical social research.

SPEED BUMPS

A Student-Friendly Guide
to Qualitative Research

INTRODUCTION

Speed bumps: raised places in the road that limit one's speed. When we are moving too fast, we must suddenly slow down or be thrown off course. Knowing that qualitative work can easily throw young (and veteran) researchers off course and that slowing down helps prevent that, we offer a set of essays in which we explore our methodological and ethical concerns as they have emerged in our recent research on urban America, research that has been generously funded by the Spencer and Carnegie foundations. We have put together this volume from a behind-the-scenes point of view in order to pry open a conversation about the *doing* of qualitative research. Across chapters, we explore issues raised as we and our graduate students engaged in the work of urban ethnographies over the past eight years.

Qualitative work has gained enormous popularity since the early 1970s as numerous journals and first-rate presses now seek to publish these materials. While there are a number of outstanding how-to books on qualitative research (Bogdan & Biklen, 1982; Bogdan & Taylor, 1975; Goetz & LeCompte, 1994; LeCompte & Schensul, 1999), there is no one volume that seeks to integrate political and ethical reflections on this work with practical suggestions for how to actually do it. This volume works like a collective diary on the techniques and ethics of our research and the research of our students.

Speed Bumps is meant to be user-friendly—a short monograph for undergraduate and graduate students that can provoke discussion in college and university classrooms about the technicalities, politics, and ethics surrounding this increasingly popular form of research. A textual friend in the midst of research, this volume offers a peek at the ways in which we have conceptualized our own research process and simultaneously renders problematic many of the steps we have taken along the way. Since our research-writing process has involved a relatively large number of graduate students at both the State University of New York at Buffalo and the City University of New York Graduate Center, these students speak here about the research process as well.

As we taught courses in Qualitative Methods, we bumped into the recognition that students needed a book on the *process* of conducting qualitative work—an honest, reflective cacophony of voices and research decisions made, mistakes and regrets, and simple, amazing moments that never make it to the final version of an article or book. So this volume represents an edited-down and pulled-together version of a set of essays that have appeared elsewhere. In Chapter 1, we offer a concrete example of our urban ethnographic work as an example of the *product*, drawing upon research involving 154 in-depth interviews with white, African American, and Latino young adults, ages 23–35, about their experiences since leaving high school. As part of a larger study (Fine & Weis, 1998), this essay inevitably glosses over both technical information regarding how we actually came to our conclusions as well as any ethical dilemmas we may have confronted along the way. In Chapter 2, we offer a standard methods note—an essay designed to let the reader know exactly how we conducted the work both to enable replication of this work and to introduce those new to qualitative research methods to ways one can go about actually doing it. In Chapters 3 and 4, we reflect back on our own work, problematizing this apparently seamless process and offering a medley of methodological and ethical concerns as we and our students experienced them. Thus we offer four slices—four lenses, if you will—on the same ethnographic whole. By compiling these essays in this fashion, we offer concrete steps through which one can conduct a piece of qualitative research and at the same time urge the reader to complexify what may appear to be a seamless whole.

We compile this book to invite student researchers into the world of qualitative work. We do not intend to render the task of qualitative work so daunting that no one will embark upon it. Between us, we have over forty years of conducting this type of research, and we can attest to the exhilaration one experiences as one does it. We do, though, wish to urge those new to the research process to take the time to think about what they are doing every step of the way, alone or with friends, colleagues, and sometimes informants. Over the past eight years we paid close attention to our research and "writing-stories," to use Laurel Richardson's term—stories that lie beneath the surface of the final product, stories that need to come out and be thought through if we are to engage in this work in a meaningful fashion. As in many cultures where the elders tell stories to the young for guidance and protection, so in this same spirit we offer these stories here.

CHAPTER I

COPS, CRIME, AND VIOLENCE

Michelle: If the President were to come to Jersey City (Buffalo) to hold a town meeting, what problems would you want him to pay attention to?

Frank: Crime and drugs, violence in the streets. The drug problem is out of hand.

All respondents were asked the question posed by the interviewer; almost all offered a response similar to Frank's. Like an urban mantra, the young men and women whom we interviewed expressed a common fear. In this chapter we try to understand not only the common experience of fear associated with crime, but also how distinct subcommunities of women and men explain the prevalence of crime, where they locate the source of the problem, and how they articulate its effects on their children's lives.

CRIME AND POVERTY

Scholarly work on crime and poverty has spawned a number of important policy and theoretical conversations about causes and also consequences, particularly in communities of highly concentrated poverty. But this literature, however brilliant, has often ignored critical facts that our interviews will reveal: that even experiences as seemingly clear-cut as *crime* and *fear* are deeply marbled by class, race, and gender.

Several main themes emerge from recent work on crime and poverty (Fagan, Conley, Debro, Curtis, Hamid, Moore, Padilla, Quicker, Taylor, & Vigil, 1993; Currie, 1993). Fagan and colleagues, in a rigorous review of available literature and a deep ethnographic look at eight urban communities across the United States, conclude that communities of concentrated poverty are today marked by what they call a break in the intergenerational linkages that in the past helped each generation find their way to stable employment and immersion in conventional life roles. To paraphrase Elijah Anderson (1990), the "old heads" are gone or no longer respected. When jobs and factories vacated urban America, unions disappeared in the urban northeast, and the tradition, which worked best for white men, of passing jobs and connections from generation to generation was threatened. The consequences of this economic, community-based bankruptcy are multiple (Currie, 1993), among them the well-established institutionalization of drug markets (Bourgois, 1995). As Bourgois notes, it is not that all inner-city residents are drug dealers, but that drug dealers now control public space, thus exerting control over inner-city life far in excess of what their numbers would predict.

Scholars also document increasing rates of violence provoked, received, and/or witnessed in communities of poverty (Hsieh & Pugh, 1993; MacLeod, 1995; Sullivan, 1989), and there is a parallel scholarship on the alarming consequences of urban violence on children and youth. A recent study documents that 40 percent of inner-city youngsters from 6th to 10th grade have witnessed a shooting or stabbing within the past year, with 74 percent reporting feeling "unsafe." It has also been shown that those children exposed to high levels of "stressful life events," including violence, are more likely to display high levels of aggression themselves (Attar, Guerra, & Tolan, 1994).

Despite its usefulness, the literature on violence does not reveal the ways in which even such supposedly clear-cut experiences as crime and fear vary dramatically by class, race, and gender. Rarely are these issues examined by demographic groups. It is assumed that we all know what crime and fear are, and that all Americans experience them in the same way. In this chapter we look at crime through the eyes and narrations of the men and women—white, African American, and Latino—with whom we worked in poor and working-class communities. We worry that research on crime and violence in poor urban America and policies stemming from this research, even at their best, have been written through a narrow, even singular, lens and therefore speak from the perspective of only some of those living within these communities. Our goal here is to de-center and complicate what we take to be a unitary representation of crime and violence, a representation which quickly crumbles when we speak across ethnic/racial and gender groups.

In this chapter, we analyze the narrative responses to three question groups:

1. Think about Jersey City (Buffalo) as it has changed over the past 12 years, particularly around crime. Do you see Jersey City (Buffalo) as more violent today than it was in the 1980s? Do you see more, less, or the same amount of what could be called police brutality?
2. There are a lot of institutions in Jersey City (Buffalo) that shape our lives—police, welfare, courts, schools, hospitals. Can you tell me about a time you had to struggle with one of these institutions for yourself or a relative? What happened?
3. There are a lot of young men in jails. How do you explain this? Why do you think this is the case?

Our data sweep us toward two conclusions. First, the experience of urban terror associated with crime, violence, and drugs is articulated passionately and profoundly by poor and working-class men and women, across racial and ethnic groups. Urban fears are democratically distributed among the poor. Second, while the terror may be universal, the *articulated site of violence* varies dramatically by demographic group. Although all informants were similar in age (23–35) and class (poor or working-class), they varied by race, ethnicity, and gender. When asked about violence in their communities, African American men and Latinos (to a far lesser extent) focused their comments on *state-initiated* violence, detailing incidents of police harassment, the systemic flight of jobs and capital from poor communities of color, the overarrest of men of color, and the revived construction of prisons. In response to the very same questions, however, white men in our study report incidents of *street violence*, attributing these incidents almost universally to men of color. In sharp contrast to all three groups of men, white women, when asked about crime and violence, offer scenes of *domestic violence* among their parents, themselves and husbands or boyfriends, or sisters and husbands or boyfriends. African American and Latino women likewise detail scenes of home-based violence, although African American women, like men from the same community, just as often describe incidents of state-initiated violence, typically in the welfare office. And African American women, like white men, passionately narrate incidents of street violence.

We hear, then, that depending on where one sits in the social hierarchy, the experience of urban fear of violence will be traced to different sources. And yet with all the national talk about crime bills, prevention and prosecution, the particular standpoint that has influenced social policy and scholarship most directly—that is, the standpoint that is best reflected in prevailing laws and academic writing—is the standpoint spoken in our data almost entirely by white men, those who discuss neither state-initiated violence, nor domestic violence; those who focus exclusively, almost fetishistically, on street violence initiated by men of color.

We introduce our data to demonstrate that the full trilogy of violence and crime—state, community, and domestic—must be taken seriously in order to be responsive to the range of needs embedded within poor and working class-communities. If national policy and social science refuse to recognize and address state-initiated violence, community violence, and domestic violence—all three—then we must cynically conclude that federal, state, and local legislation is being written in ways that reflect prevalently the terrors, needs, and projections of white males while silencing the voices of men and women of color as well as white women in their cries for violence-free homes and communities.

Our data will show that living in communities of concentrated poverty, now exacerbated by a drug economy in which individuals are armed with easy access to guns, has many consequences: the material well-being of community members has diminished; little to no trust exists between adults—reducing the ability to depend on a neighbor for support, help, assistance, or information; children are often locked in their homes, unable to play outside, limited physically, socially, and psychologically—gluing them and their mothers to television as a dominant transmitter of social beliefs and world views; and women and children are unable to take advantage of the few educational, social, or recreational programs that may still exist because they fear for their lives.

Reviewing responses to the questions listed above and using grounded theory, we targeted various themes: (a) *focus* of the violence—that is, state, community, domestic; (b) *trust* in the police; (c) whether or not the respondent speaks in a *racialized discourse*; (d) whether or not the respondent indicated that the *police advised* him or her about how to "take justice into my own hands"; (e) whether the respondent sees *police brutality* on the rise, decline, or stabilized over the past decade. Using these themes as our lens, we hear quite distinct stories pouring out of each demographic category: white men, white women, black men, black women, Latinos and Latinas. Torn by the desire not to essentialize, we are nevertheless forced by our data to recognize the ways in which violence operates through race, class, and gender. For a cursory look, see Table 1.1; we review the data by demographic groups and then we speak across groups.[1]

Table 1.1. Views of Violence and the Police Across Demographic Groups

	White Men	White Women	African American Men	African American Women	Latinos	Latinas
Focus of Violence	*Community* Focus on street violence perpetrated by "other"	*Domestic* Focus on gender	*State* Focus on racist implementation of policies	*State, street, and domestic* Focus on race and gender	*State* Focus on race	*Domestic* Focus on gender
Views of Police	Friends; family; high trust	Moderate trust	High mistrust; corruption	Mistrust	Mistrust	High mistrust; corruption

DEMOGRAPHIC STORIES

White Men

Of the six groups, white men emerged as the most distinct, that is, atypical, narrators. A full half of these men spontaneously volunteered that they had a friend or relative who is a "cop." Quite distinct from the rest of the sample, 75 percent indicated high levels of trust in the police, and only 25 percent alluded to police corruption in a city in which 75 percent of Latinos and African American men reported instances of corruption and police brutality. Alan says:

> Oh, the police. Well I, last week when we had the break-in, the police came down. I thought it was kind of strange, you know, that the one cop said to me that it was too bad that you didn't catch him inside the house because then you could have killed him and we wouldn't have said anything. He said it was too bad I didn't catch him, I could have beat the crap out of him. But I don't really think I've had a run-in, so to speak.

As one can hear, Alan feels protected by the police. Like Alan, three other white men independently volunteered that the police, following their reporting of a crime, instructed them in how to "get the guy" next time. Along with declaring their trust in the police, these men insisted on identifying the race of perpetrators. It is noteworthy that the white men were the only group who insisted on naming the race/ethnicity of their perpetrators—or at least naming those who were black or Latino.

When discussing fears, white men consistently projected fear onto others—parents, children, sisters—while denying their personal fears. In other words, white men would narrate a racialized discourse of crime and punishment, attributing virtue and responsibility to the police who represent "us," criminality and degradation to men of color, all the while discussing this in terms of protecting elders, women, and children. In this triangle, these men do not see police brutality. Or they do not, in the words of one, "see enough." A full 75 percent indicated that police brutality was on the wane or that allegations of police brutality were nothing more than fabrications—again unusual in a city in which most of our respondents recited incidents of personal and/or witnessed acts of brutality. Sixty percent of white men considered charges of police harassment to be "racially trumped up." These men, more than other groups, narrated an empathy with police officers, sometimes combined with a dismissal of harassment charges, other times honestly conflicted. Bob, for example, offers the following analysis of police brutality:

> I don't know. I mean police brutality is such a crock sometimes. Most of the time people that are getting brutalized have done something one way or another to intimidate the police officer. He [police officer] doesn't have the easiest job in the world, so it's tough to say what's brutality and what's not. I mean there's instances when innocent people do get roughed up, too, but unfortunately that's because of the violence that's out there. Police are no longer reacting with any courtesy. They're just grabbing people, and that's because of what they have to face. Anybody could potentially be a killer in a policeman's eyes. It don't matter if you're ten or a hundred. So that's what they have to live with. Forty hours a week they have to worry about that. From the second they start to the second they finish, there's not really a time when they can't worry about it, so that's a big problem. You say "Are police too rough?" What about the people, are the people too rough? Is there, like, civilian brutality towards the police? Are they allowed to do whatever they want? I don't think so. I think there's some type of law you have to uphold.

White Women

Unlike white men, fewer than half of the white women "trust" the police; 60 percent narrate stories of police and courts in terms of violence in their homes, or in the homes of their mothers and their sisters. They, too, see little in the way of brutality, but 48 percent of those interviewed recognize corruption in the ranks. Many express the kind of frustration with police evident in this account by Caroline:

> Well, like with my sister, my middle sister. She lived with a boyfriend who was a drug addict. Well, he was reformed and then he moved in with her and he was, the present one. And he became a problem. My parents were away and he was, you know, threatening my sister and stuff. And he locked us in the house and he was threatening to kill us, and all this sick stuff. So anyway, we had to call the police about eight times that day. And they had to arrest him. But it was, I mean, as far as the police go, it was a very ... it was frustrating at first and then, then it was a good experience because they helped us. You know, they protected us. At one point I didn't think they were going to, and I really was going a little bit crazy, you know. They kept sending him on his way and he kept coming back, you know ... And I started screaming, you know. I'm like, "you're giving him change [money] and sending him on his way? He'll be back in an hour. Where is this guy going with a crack problem and a dollar?" You know, so I'm, like, screaming at this cop and everything. And then the other two came and, you know, I was pleading with this, the one who came back. I was like, "you swore you were going to put him in jail. My sister and me are scared to death. My father isn't here." We have nobody, you know.

Because the police potentially protect women from violent men, these women, unlike the women of color, see the police as "responsive." Indeed one woman who had her husband locked up for domestic violence and brought him to court on charges of nonpayment of child support, describes working with neighbors on a petition to get more police protection. In line with the fact that white women only whisper about incidents of domestic violence which pervade their lives, they tend not to call the cops, take out restraining orders, or bring their husbands to court. Most of the white women, in fact, have had few dealings with the police. They are still more likely than their white brothers to note police imperfections, and yet more likely than women of color to trust them.

Cecilia: We had a situation where these people were coming from Duncan Projects, harassing the neighborhood kids. And what we did

was we called up the North District Police Department and we
asked to have them drive through occasionally because the kids were
being harassed. They were being robbed and everything else, and at
first it was, like, a problem, but then we got like this big list, I think it
was like 4,000 people.

Sarah: Oh, a petition?

Cecilia: Yeah, and we brought it up to them and we got it [protection].

Sarah: 4,000 people. Wow. Who did that?

Cecilia: Well, me, this girl Brenda, we went through the buildings.

Sarah: Do you think it is important to do this kind of work?

Cecilia: Yeah, because you see, if you don't protect what you have, nobody
is going to protect it for you. If you show, if you just move in and you
see that other parents are interested in everybody else's kids as well as
their own, you feel more comfortable knowing that someone is looking
for your kids, too. So then you say, I'm going to look for their kids.

Sarah: The police are responsive to your needs?

Cecilia: Oh yeah, they are, yeah, they are. At first it was a little bit of a
problem because they said they don't have enough cars. So we just
blew it off and they thought it was over with, but then we went and
had the petition made and brought it to the Commissioner and it
was over with. We got it taken care of.

African American Men

In our interviews with African American men, we heard two powerful
discourses of violence. One was what we might call the everyday work of
counter hegemony for and by black men—working against the violence of
racist representations. In the constant confrontation with harsh and humili-
ating public representations of their race, ethnicity, class, gender, and sexuality, understanding full well the images of black men constructed and
distributed by the media and popular culture, these black men battle their
image as criminal, as super athlete, as super entertainer.

The second discourse of violence spoken by black men is their powerful, incisive, and painful social critique. When African American men speak
of violence, their analyses move directly to economic and state violence.
What we encounter through these interviews is a group of men deeply
concerned about the fate of their community. Surrounded by street-based
violence and drugs, as well as the violence perpetrated by police in their

communities, African American men voice a deep systemic critique targeting the lack of jobs, racism, and police harassment.

Thus, for instance, when asked about violence in his community, Jon, an African American gay man, poses a caustic analysis of political violence:

> The top people that control the society, they're the most angry, violent people in the world. They drop bombs. They spread diseases. They burn. They set up armies to do all kinds of things. I don't know all the violence that you talkin' about. Frankly, I don't see it. People stab each other. They always have. You know, so I see it, but it's just magnified on the television, but they don't show the real violence that they perpetrate, the economic violence.

In marked contrast to the white men, the African American men do not (with one exception, whose father is a police sergeant) describe police as friends or relatives. They do not trust the police. In fact, 75 percent relay stories of corruption. Most think that brutality has gotten worse in the past decade and almost all see a primary reason for the increase in the proportion of men in jail as attributable to both the economy and intensified state violence. Of the African American men interviewed, almost all reported a story in which he was stopped, frisked, or pulled over for no apparent reason. Some of the stories were told with fiery anger; others with a bitter sense of disgust and resignation. Carl, a "church-going man," recalls one incident:

> In regard to police, we hear about police brutality and I really don't allow for police brutality when it comes to me. I remember one experience when I had my car stolen and I had gotten the car back. And over a year my car was never taken off [the list] as stolen, all right. So I would call the police or whatever, trying to get it taken off. No one would help me. So I had gotten pulled over because I made a wrong turn one time, and I think you get a ticket for that. [laughs] I was pulled over. I gave him my license and registration. He was going to arrest me because he said my license was suspended. I said no. My license, well, there was something on my, whatever they said, whatever code they use, there was something on my record in regards to my driving. And I said no. My car was stolen and it has not been taken off. That can be the only thing on my driving record. All right. And so it took him a long time, you know. And he threatened me about taking and impounding my car and, you

know, this other stuff. And then all of a sudden three other cop cars pull up, stop, surround me basically, all right. Then they push me, one guy, one cop tries to put me into the cop car and I'm telling them, "I'm not," I said, "I'm not going in this cop car because I've done nothing wrong . . ."

Demetrius, another calm, church-going civil servant, relays a memory of a car accident:

I told her [friend] to stay in the car and take the keys out of my ignition. So she stayed in the car, and the next thing I know I'm walking back across the highway. I went to the grass and sidewalk, and the next thing I know a car came out of nowhere, all right? And he didn't have his headlights on. So all I hear is the engine, and it's pitch black out there, and I got another 50 yards to go before I get up under a streetlight. And I'm on a sidewalk, and the car's on the sidewalk. The car brushes by my leg, and we're on grass, and if he would have slightly lost control of that car, he would have took my leg out, okay? The car just slid right past me. I was actually running across the street to get to the sidewalk, and that's when it happened. He jumps out of the car and he came to me . . . and asked me if I wanted to fight. And my question was, "Why?" And he started cursing and everything, calling me all kinds of names, and so by then I'm getting mad. And so he approached me and he pushed me, he pushed me in the chest. So I backed up, and he's like, "What, you want to fight, black boy, you want a fight?" And I backed up and, well, I guess there's no alternative, you know? So he took a swing at me, right, and I blocked it, and I was going to hit him back, and he reached in his pocket and pulled out a gun. That was my first experience of actually seeing a gun up close, and he pointed it right at my head. And I didn't know what to do, all right? So I just put my hands up nice and slow. I said, "what's going on?" Just like that. And he was like, "I'm a police officer," like that, right, "I should run your big behind in," all this stuff. I'm like, "What are you talking about?" He was like, he's carrying on and carrying on, but he wasn't telling me what he was doing. All of a sudden, you know, he's a man with a gun. That what I see him as. I don't see him as a police officer. He didn't show me no badge. It's Halloween night. I don't know who's out here perpetrating that they were a cop.

Even Paul, whose father is a police sergeant, who explains that the "police have a job to do," notes, "If I go into a white neighborhood, I get stopped." These men repeat story after story of being suspect and narrate the toll that it takes. He explains: "White women are scared of black men. It makes you feel cheap." Paul is asked what he tells his children about police, and he hesitates, thinks, and then answers:

Paul: Well, [my] son, he loved policemen and cops and all this stuff. So, I'll let him see when he gets older, but now, I'll tell him the cops are good and when you are in trouble, call the police or an ambulance.
Michelle: So you do tell him?
Paul: I don't shatter his dreams. 'Cause he says he wants to get to be a cop when he grows older, like, okay. You know.
Michelle: Do you think it would shatter him?
Paul: If they're still going where they're going now, yeah, it will be shattered. Or if he have a struggle, I'll just focus on the other people, and don't be like the other cops, like the way they are now.

Black men are not only far more structural in their explanations of the root causes of crime and corruption, but they are far more devastated and hard put than other groups to imagine how to turn things around. Many note, with regret, the absence of community-based programs, the slashing of budgets for after-school programs. John remembers, fondly, that his community used to care for all the children, and now he's scared. "The neighbors used to be so nosey," but now "I don't know what to do to stop the violence." The black men whom we interviewed were critical of the "system," concerned about state and street violence, and beleaguered in their attempts to help the "young ones, still comin' up."

Stuart: The neighborhood isn't as close as it used to be. Everybody used to be nosey, as a way of saying it in street talk. You know, if something's happening, you would hear windows going up throughout the neighborhood, and now you don't hear it, everybody is keeping to themselves. And if somebody's getting beat up or something outside, or if there is a crime taking place, they're sheltered, they don't open windows as much, you know, because they're scared they might get a bullet, you know, or something like that. As when, back when I was growing up, my mother, if she seen somebody next door or around the corner, one of my friends doing something like that, they weren't supposed to do, she had the permission to get involved and, you know, chastise the person if they were doing wrong, and that's the same as me. Like, if I was around in somebody else's neighborhood, and they knew my parents, I knew not to do anything wrong because I knew that they were watching over me.

Judi: So do you yourself, if you see something wrong now, are you likely to get involved, or are you not likely to get involved?

Stuart: I just recently got involved with something. I wasn't able to stop what happened. A guy in my neighborhood that's my sister's friend, he was literally beat down with baseball bats and, you know, I just helped him out as far as getting him towels and ice and stuff like that, calling the police and ambulance. But I think that if I would have seen him actually doing it, I probably would have gotten involved. You know, I hate to see my neighborhood get, you know, get to total destruction like a lot of other neighborhoods that I've seen.

Judi: So you feel partly responsible for it?

Stuart: Partly responsible, exactly.

African American Women

The black women we interviewed, like the black men, do not trust the police much. While 25 percent think the cops are corrupt and 25 percent report dealings with police in scenes of domestic violence, they are, overall, tired of picking up the pieces for white society and for African American men. These women narrate stories of exhaustion, few resources, fewer supports. They cast the widest net around their dealings with the law, noting landlord-tenant cases, child support, restraining orders, and run-ins with caseworkers. Genette's fatigue with all parts of the system is clear in the following:

> So I said, "All right, you can see the baby, you want to come see him, you can come see him, but just know, me and you, we have no business with each other except for this child. Don't touch me, don't act like you want me," I said, "cause I don't want you." I don't know, he came like for three times, he came like every other day, he would come for like three visits, so the last day, he talkin' about, oh, "I don't want you on welfare." I said, "well, wait a minute, you don't have a job," and then at the time he was about to go to jail and I said, so, "How is my baby gonna get taken care of, how my baby gonna go to the doctor and everything," I said, "unless the system help me until I could get back to work?" "No, no, I don't want my baby on welfare," and this and that. I said, "Well, it's too late, because he's on it," so he gets mad at me. I said, "Well, you're

the man, you go get a job now before you go to jail and you take him." I said, "and then you talk about the rest later," you know what I'm sayin', because the only reason why he didn't want me dealing with welfare because he knew the system would say, who the father is, and they would take him to court, so he didn't want to go to the process of having to pay child support.

Stories of male violence are not as frequent as they are for white and Latino women, but they are dramatic and devastating in consequence.

Tara: Yeah. The time he was trying to hurt me, and I knew that he didn't want to hurt me, you know, to try to kill me. And when the judge asked me that, he didn't ask me that personally, he just said, "Tara, do you have anything to say about the situation?" And I didn't talk. I was scared. It was like [John] took over me. I didn't, I had just talked my piece. He wasn't a ruler over me. I just took it like I didn't have nothing to say.

Sarah: Let's go back, okay. You pressed charges . . .

Tara: This was years ago. Like five, maybe six years ago. He burnt my door and wouldn't let me out the door. And my brother and them came and moved the chair, and I got out.

Sarah: I understand that. Why did he do that?

Tara: To scare me. Remember I told you he been trying to scare me. I think I did tell you . . .

Sarah: Did you call anybody? What did you do, cry?

Tara: Cry. I panicked.

Sarah: And what happened?

Tara: I just got down on all fours . . . [laughs]

Sarah: And prayed?

Tara: Yeah. And woke up my kids. And . . .

Sarah: Your kids were inside too?

Tara: Yeah, all of us. And we all got down on all fours and sat in the house for fifteen minutes before the fire department came.

The African American women with whom we spoke—even before "welfare reform"—were typically holding together their own families and caring for the children or parents of kin, and doing so with meager resources. Their anger at the police is matched by their anger at African American men, caseworkers, African American women who "make us look bad," and the younger generation who are committing crimes and thereby rendering their neighborhoods terrifying for women and children. These women speak through a dual discourse of responsibility and blame. More than one quoted, "You do the crime, you do the time." More than one alluded to a domestic cycle of drugs, violence, *his* doing time . . . and then *his* not paying child support.

Black women experience brutality in their own homes, witness it in neighbors', worry that their primary obligation is to their children. "I don't get involved." There is little regret in this sentence for the women, for they know that if they do "get involved," that is, call the cops on a neighbor's domestic violence, they are vulnerable to retaliation. They live amidst and despite violence, knowing they and their children are ever vulnerable . . . and so they are ever vigilant. From the eye of this hurricane, their anger is tempered by vulnerability. Violence keeps them in their homes, and scared.

Latino Men (Latinos)

Also parting ways with the white men, and sounding more like their African American brothers, 100 percent of the Latinos in Jersey City remarked on high levels of police corruption in the city. This is in contrast with Latinos in Buffalo, where a critique of police does not surface as forcefully.[2] One has a friend on the police force. One says he trusts the cops. Two cited incidents of domestic violence, involving mothers and sisters. Latinos, like the Latinas, see family problems as the primary predictor of men going to jail. They see police brutality everywhere, with the "police thinking they are above the law."

Andy: That's interesting. Do you see any kind of thing about, like, police brutality? Do you . . .

Pablo: Uh, yes. Some of the police get me angry because, in [supermarket] we have a police officer there and they're there from five to eleven. I've finally, over the past five years or so, started to get to know them, and they know me by first-name basis or give me a Police Benevolent Association card or, you know, now we talk to them. But what gets you mad is now that they know me, they let down their guard, and . . .

Andy: What kind of conversations do you have?

Pablo: And they'll just have, you know, all types of conversations, you know, this scum was doing this, and the way they term people, that you already know they already have a bad outlook towards someone to begin with. And you'll have like two officers in front of me talking and he goes, "Yeah, I went to a Flores house, and he was talking about this and I told him to shut up, and he didn't say nothing. I stand on the floor and kicked him," and this and that, "Are you gonna shut up now," and you're looking at the, and you just say to yourself, you know, I feel like I'm gonna report this guy or whatever, but what can I get done because then I've seen so many officers that have something reported on them and there's like a system you're not gonna, unless you get something like a Rodney King that's on video tape, the possibility of a police officer getting in trouble for doing something like that is rare.

Luis resonated to the desire to be useful amidst violence in a war zone. He sounds like the African American men when he said:

Oh, the police. They really think they're above the law. And they do what they want, and they get away with it. They really do. There's no way you can say it. The guy who got hung, they beat this guy when he had handcuffs, at the county jail? There were too many riots, protests going, so they closed the jail down and moved [the jail] to Kearney. All the prisoners. Those police officers, don't do that again. That's all they got. There was a trial, the family was suing them. It got thrown out of court. Those cops are going to turn around and do the same thing to somebody else. The police, definitely less police brutality now than before. I think in part because they're scared. Because if they hit somebody, that person might have a gun, or their friend might have a gun that will shoot them. So there's more like, this noncaring attitude, it's like, do what you want, do what you want. That's why I personally went and got a gun, but it's registered. And it sits right by my window. At night, if anything happens, the cars are parked right there, I won't hesitate to shoot. Because I'm sick of this place basically. The way it's going. I want to save it, but I don't know what to do.

Latino Women (Latinas)

By far the most pronounced critique of the police comes from the Latinas who are, like African American women, profoundly disappointed in both the police and in their men. In both instances they expect a lot and get little.

Their disappointment with the police is much like their experience with domestic violence. Despite the violence—repeated and severe—they maintain a faith in family, heterosexuality, and marriage that is sacred and unwavering. A full 75 percent of the Latinas believe the police are corrupt and violent, and an equal percentage have come into contact with police because of incidents of domestic violence. These women often know how to get the police to do what they need to do, aware of the racial politics that must be maneuvered in order to get the cops to respond.

Marta believes that the cops "don't care. When it comes to domestic violence in our community, they think, 'Let them kill themselves.'"

Mun: What were the issues of the community, you were saying?

Marta: Like I see the cops go by, and they see the kids in the corner, and sometimes they'll say something and sometimes they won't. You know, like they look the other way. You call 911 and say, "Okay. I'm calling from such and such a building. There's kids hanging outside. It's 3 o'clock in the morning. I can't sleep." The cops won't come. They won't come. They will never show up. Or, there's a domestic fight in apartment such and such. You'll sit there and die before they come. I mean the wife will be dead, and he'll beat her to death, before the cops ever come.

Mun: Because they don't want, because they don't care? Or because they don't want to walk in that neighborhood? Or because?

Marta: I think it's both of them. I think it's just like, this society, I think the way they see it is, let them kill themselves. They'll take care of themselves. You know, black people killing black people. The Latinos are killing each other. They're killing, they both take care of finishing, of terminating each other. I guess the cops just let them do it, you know. If they see two, if they see a white person and a black person fighting, they'll stop it. But if they see a Hispanic and a black person going at it they'll, you know, they'll let it happen. If you call because there's a robbery, they'll let it happen. If you call because it's a domestic fight, they'll let it happen. . . . The cops, they are a joke, the cops. And most of the cops know the kids, and most of the cops, how can I tell you? The cops will tell them, "Look, I'm going to let you go this time. But next time I'm going to do something to you." And they really don't do anything. And some of the times, the cops are the ones who are dealing with them. You know, so it's inside jobs. And sometimes you see the cops talking to the kids outside. And the kids will tell you, "No, man, he's with us. He's with us." So you have no type of police protection at all, at all. I mean, if you, if you would live where I live and you order a Blimpie, they will not take it to your apartment. You have to come outside and get it. Because they will not go in there. If you order a pizza, they will, they'll give you a hard time going into my neighborhood. "Where on Jewett?" "Bergen Avenue." "Well, can you come and meet us outside?" Because they will not, they won't go up. They won't go up. You have to go outside and get your food and then go upstairs.

Latinas, like white women, come into contact with cops, crime, and violence around issues of domestic violence.

Carmen: Yeah, that's why I would like to be a cop. Because, like, my brother is so terrible, I could, you know, just ...

Mun: Who, Ray?

Carmen: Yeah. I could just control him and whoever gets, my sister's husband hit her, I'd get in and, you know, control them, too. So I would like to be a cop. I like, let me see what kind of cop. I would like to be the ones that go when there's problems. They go to an apartment ...

Mun: Domestic violence and stuff?

Carmen: Yeah. That's what I would like.

Mun: If somebody, some husband is beating some wife, you would go in there?

Carmen: Yeah. I want them to feel how she'll feel ... No, he doesn't beat me. He only screams and he grabs me through my neck, but he doesn't smack me. He doesn't hit me with a bat.

Mun: How come your neighbor called the police?

Carmen: No, my brother.

Mun: He called the police?

Carmen: Yeah, but it was, I told him to look, the other time I called the cops and he just left in front of the door, so I told my brother, that's what they gonna do now, so my brother told me, no, watch, and he called the cops. So I had to go forward with it. He called the cops and what I'm gonna tell the cops, "Go, I don't need you."

Tamar: Because he was doing all the screaming and punching and she was the one doing all the crying, so you could tell. And I called the cops and said bring, you know, can you send me a car, there are kids involved, the man is hitting, and I said please hurry up, and I was polite. She was telling me, she was a black lady, and I'm like, but there are kids involved, you know, and I gave the information, so she wanted to have my name, and I told her, "I'm not gonna give you my name," and she's like, "Well, if you don't give me the name, I'm not gonna send the cops." So I told her, "If you don't send the cops, somehow there's gonna be a recording that I did call you and you didn't do anything about it," so, you know, and I hung up.

Mun: Did the police come?

Tamar: Yeah, they came. They came in less than three minutes. If it wouldn't have been for me, forget it.

Mun: How did that make you feel?

Tamar: It gave me flashbacks of me. And I wish that when they heard me screaming, somebody would have called the cops or knock on my door and tell me if I'm alright, they don't do that. . . .

Mun: Why do you think some men are beating up women? We hear a lot about this.

Margarita: Excuse me, why do they beat their wives? I guess because that makes them in control. That's the only person they can control, maybe, you know, because, that's why I say sometimes, like, to the baby's father, don't be yelling at me, why don't you go and, go do that to a man outside and see what happens. You'll get punched right in the face. You know, cause sometimes it's true, you haven't done nothing to that person and they come and they, you know, treating you bad, and you say, Wait a minute, what happened? And I say like that, "Don't talk to me like that, or treat me like that. You have an apartment, go to whoever gave you the problem, see, and do that face to face," you know, cause they'll slap the shit out of you, or whatever, you know. But I think it's that, it's that they, control, that they can control you or, yeah, control. . . . [Referring to her sister's boyfriend] I think he went to jail for a couple of . . . He was only a week or two days, something like that. She, she has no say in that and, and, instead of, I don't know if she, but sometimes those things don't work, getting, um, what is it these things?

Mun: Injunction?

Margarita: Injunctions to, those things don't work. It just doesn't work.

Mun: Why?

Margarita: That's why a lot of, I don't know, that's why, because I guess
    when a man sets his mind to do something, a little piece of paper is
    not gonna stop him, and I don't think even the police is gonna stop
    him. I think when they set their minds to, they're [men] gonna do
    this, they're gonna hurt you or they're gonna do this, they're gonna
    do it.

Restraining orders have little effect, according to the women we talked
with, and many women think the police are prejudiced by virtue of race/
ethnicity and gender. And yet, with all the violence Latinas report in their
families of origin and families of procreation, their commitments to *familia*
and fears of escape and retaliation run very deep.

VIOLENCE IN POOR COMMUNITIES

From our data, we hear poor and working-class young adults in the grips
of violence. But we also hear the tilting influence of their relative position
in analyzing this violence. So, for instance, we understand that all residents
whom we interviewed carry around fears of violence and see police as very
powerful players. For the white men, however, police are *protectors* of community, whereas for people of color, and some of the white women, police
are *perpetrators* of personal and community abuse. This, too, speaks clearly
to questions of policy. If police are not trusted broadly, if they do not represent multiple voices, do not come from and represent the demographic
and neighborhood groups and interests of all community members, if they
are, or appear to be, unconcerned with violence within neighborhoods of
color while far more responsive when the caller is white, we need ways to
reimagine and redesign community policing so that the level of respon-
siveness and the time of arrival are not calculated through racism and
institutional neglect.

We began our data analysis committed to an analytic strategy that
would cut across these demographic groups. We intended to look for any
apparent "differences" evident in demographic contrasts, but were determined *not* to organize our analyses around these differences. And yet our
data surprised us, as powerful data often do, forcing us to recognize the
material and experiential consequences of particular race/ethnicity and
gender positions in the United States. While the women and men we inter-

viewed pledged the irrelevance of race/ethnicity and gender—"I don't think about it much"—their stories are saturated with such evidence. Race, class, and gender *are* socially constructed—and deeply engraved.

So we conclude this chapter with a set of chilling reflections on cops, crime, and violence. After analyzing our narratives, we must admit that the public policies and institutions we perhaps naively assumed were clear-cut ended up being much more fluid, interpretable, multiple, and transitory than we expected. So, for instance, notions of community, cops, violence, and crime were revealed as not at all concrete entities with clear referents. Instead, these turned out to be highly negotiated and personally interpreted relationships, developed over history, within racial and gendered politics, in quite local and specific contexts. These policies and institutions perform quite differently for different groups. In contrast to our initial sense that demography was fleeting but social institutions concrete, our data suggest just the reverse. In poor communities, demography is more biographically engraved than we would wish. And social institutions are quite discriminating in daily experience.

Every interviewee was aware of and frightened by violence and crime. But the commonality stops there. For African American men, their most pronounced fears involve state violence. And, indeed, Jersey City and Buffalo Criminal Index data show a dramatic spike in drug arrests from 1985 forward, particularly for African Americans, which is perplexing given national surveys which indicate equal levels of drug use for whites and African Americans (U.S. Department of Justice, 1995). The vigilance for arrests, and black arrests in particular, has peaked, as have the imprisonment rates. So while 13 percent of monthly drug users are African American, 35 percent of drug related arrests, 55 percent of convictions, and 74 percent of prison sentences involve African Americans. (Data are for 1992 and 1993 depending on the most recent available figures.) For white men, their worries focus specifically on racially choreographed street violence. And, indeed, the Criminal Index indicates a rise in robbery, rape, assault, burglary, and larceny from 1975–1990 in both Jersey City and Buffalo. For women across racial/ethnic groups, their terrors surround domestic violence; national data suggest that women across racial/ethnic groups suffer roughly equivalent rates of violence, with low-income women far more susceptible to intimate violence than middle-class or upper-class women. We assert, then, in terms of policy recommendations, that a federal, state, or local crime policy must address simultaneously all three kinds of violence—state violence, community violence, and domestic violence. These three work as a set, a triplet, a collection of interrelated and embodied experiences of social life in poor and working-class communities. And as a set, they affect children and youth—the next generation—with devastating predictability, whether these children are witnesses, victims, or, for some, perpetrators of the violence.

A NOTE ON BLAME

As a chapter epilogue we offer some commentary about the discourses that community members deploy when they talk about crime, violence, and responsibility. We do this in order to right a set of publicly advertised misconceptions. While the popular media continue to paint degenerated pictures of poor communities of color, our data paint a very different picture.

Indeed the only group committed to an analysis of violence in which they take no responsibility for the growth of violence is white men. With some exceptions, white men, as a group, identified the source of the "problem" to be men of color. The "solution," for white men, is the containment or confinement of these same men. In contrast, the most pronounced discourse of responsibility could be heard from the African American women, who are the most likely to see criminal behavior as an outcome of bad personal choices and irresponsibility and the least likely to offer up macro-structural explanations for why young black men are so heavily over-represented in jails and prisons today. That is, African American women tended not to assert that the absence of jobs, the presence of racism, or hard economic times contribute to high rates of imprisonment. Because these women see entire communities as vulnerable to these conditions, they are unwilling with any regularity to attribute criminal behavior to these structural conditions. They assert, instead, with remarkable consistency that "if you commit the crime, you do the time." No fancy explanations or justifications. "If my children can struggle out here and stay out of jail—so can the others." A discourse of responsibility, perhaps even blame, is articulated most unambivalently from these women.

In analytic contrast with their African American sisters, African American men in both cities and Latinos in Jersey City assert broad-based structural explanations for why their men are overpopulating jails these days. Offering theories of "conspiracy," the "system," corruption, recession, no jobs, and racism, these men are not, however, shirking responsibility. Quite a few end their discussions of crime and violence with a sobering sense of personal powerlessness. Filled with a desire to create change, they voice frustration that few avenues are available. We remember the words of Luis who sits by his window with gun in hand, wanting to do something, but not knowing what.

CONCLUDING THOUGHTS

The mid-1990s have marked a painful moment in racial history. We are reminded often and sharply of the enormous racial and class divides that continue to define community life in America. We watch helplessly as Congress passes legislation which demonizes people of color and people in poverty. We listen in relative silence, if not collusion, as these women and men are blamed for their own conditions.

Our data suggest a picture of social, racial, and class relations quite distinct from those drawn by Congress. We hear women and men of the poor and working classes, white, black and Latino, disappointed by public and personal institutions ranging from welfare to the family to public schools, in pain about personal and collective tragedies but searching for ways to hold families together, protect communities, and take back their streets. While white men are filled disproportionately with a discursive venom that is difficult to hear, we read even their words as evidence of the pain of losing ground in an economy that has assaulted all members of the poor and working classes with only moderate benefits accruing to once protected whites.

We hear further that crime bills that would simply arrest, prosecute, and incarcerate, build more jails, cut school budgets, and deny job training will satisfy or assist no one—not even poor and working-class white men. The depth and consequence of social violence is enormous and multifaceted. Street violence is a concern for white men, indeed, and it endangers even more profoundly the mobility and public life of poor and working-class women and men of color. But for women and men of color, state violence, police harassment, false arrests, the planting of evidence, exaggerated charges, and differential sentencing policies also figure prominently in their narrations of violence. And for many of the women, there is no respite from street violence. Going home is no safer, and perhaps even more terrifying, than walking the streets at night. And leaving a violent home is no assurance of peace.

The news is not good. Our communities are fractured, and we come together frequently in fear, sometimes in finger-pointing. But, we would assert, public policies that speak largely from a privileged standpoint as if race and gender neutral—incarcerating men and women from oppressed racial groups, at unprecedented rates—contribute to the fracturing. There are policy answers for reinventing community and safety among our differences. Some of our respondents spoke of multiracial/multiethnic coalitions, petition drives and local organization across race and ethnicity, within class, between genders. The question, today, is not what to do, but who is going to listen?

CHAPTER 2

A NOTE ON METHODS

Data for *The Unknown City* (some of which appear in the preceding chapter; Fine & Weis, 1998) were collected primarily by means of in-depth interviews and focus-group interviews. Desiring to find out how regular people, who constitute the poor and working classes, view contemporary social policies, prospects for work and education, satisfying family and spiritual life, and engaging community involvement and social activism, we constructed an open-ended interview schedule that tapped a number of substantive areas. In consultation with a set of graduate students and social activists, we developed a set of interview questions, which were then pretested in the field and revised as necessary. Questions targeted issues relating to neighborhood, schooling, experience with jobs, family, gender relations, violence, social activism, religion, racial and ethnic identification, children, and desires for the future, both one's own future and that of the children. The questions were open-ended, designed to encourage interviewees to talk about their experiences in these areas. All interviewers were extensively trained in qualitative techniques of investigation, with ongoing meeting and consultation as we moved through the interviews.

We adopted a quasi–life history approach in which a series of in-depth, two- to five-hour interviews were conducted with young people, ages 23–35, of varying racial and ethnic backgrounds in order to ascertain how these groups conceptualize and experience education, employment, and family in Jersey City and Buffalo. This research was designed to hear from young men and women who survive in the working-class and poor segments of our society, how they spin images of their personal and collective futures, how they conceptualize the shrinking public and private sectors, and how they reflect upon progressive social movements that have historically and dramatically affected their ancestors' own life chances and those of their children. Even though policies are written today *for* the poor and working classes, we have yet to hear from them. Our goal, then, was to unearth the "voices" of people usually not heard and to excavate these voices across a range of life's activities.

We drew from a sample of young adults who have basically "followed the social rules" (attended school, sometimes beyond high school), focusing on people who were connected to "meaningful urban communities." We selected communities, defined not by geographic location alone (given what Wilson, 1987, and Fine & Cook, 1991, found about the lack of connection and trust in low-income urban communities) but also by meaningful social connections. Our goal was to generate a broad analysis of the "coming of age in urban America" during the 1980s and 1990s. We focused, in both cities, on four sets of urban institutions: (1) schools and postsecondary institutions, (2) churches and spiritual sites, (3) social agencies and self-help groups, and (4) community centers and activist organizations. All individuals whom we interviewed were involved in at least one of these institutions. So, for example, white, African American, and Latino men and women were drawn as equally as possible from across the four sectors in each city. Schools refer to either their children's schools or, in some cases, their own. Churches that serve the poor and working classes tend to be Catholic in urban northeastern white communities, Baptist or Holiness in the black communities, and Catholic or Pentecostal in Latino communities. Social agencies refer to agencies that actively seek (and receive funding) to train and place those who attend their programs in literacy, job training, public assistance, or domestic violence. Community centers can at times double as social agencies but primarily serve as spaces in which communities are drawn together, such as a well-known community arts center located in the fruit belt in Buffalo, parental groups, lesbian/gay centers, and theater projects. In spite of our desires, it was not possible to come up with exactly equivalent numbers in each category. White men, for example, are underrepresented in social agencies because they tend to attend in fewer numbers than the other groups, and Latinos are overrepresented in community centers, due to the prominence of particular community centers in the communities in which we worked. All in all, 154 black, white, and Latino men and women were interviewed across the two cities (see Table 2.1). Over half of the Latinos/Latinas were interviewed in Spanish, that being their language of choice for the interview.

Table 2.1. Interviewees by City, Gender, and Race/Ethnicity

	African American		White		Latino	
	Male	Female	Male	Female	Male	Female
Buffalo	18	15	13	15	11	10
Jersey City	12	16	14	12	7	11

Lists of potential institutions within each of the four target categories were drawn up and particular institutions were selected within each category, by racial and ethnic group and gender. We went and met virtually all of the gatekeepers at each institution, explaining the purpose of the project and enlisting their help. Gatekeepers provided us with the actual names of interviewees and, whenever possible, their phone numbers or other ways to locate them (not all the people had phones). Once we had a list of names, we used the "snowball effect" in order to obtain additional names. One of us or our graduate students contacted all individuals directly and set up interview times. Interviews were generally held at the institution from which their names had been obtained. Thus, interviews were conducted in churches, city schools, Head Start centers, social agencies, and various community centers.

We all fanned out through Buffalo and Jersey City, working intensely with select institutions and the individuals we contacted. Interviews were generally conducted in two segments, spanning two to five hours total. Individual interviews took place over an eighteen-month period. Each interviewee was paid $40 for the interview. All interviews were tape-recorded, with explicit conversations about confidentiality, anonymity, privacy, and informed consent. The tape recorder was fully visible on the table, and all interviewees were invited to turn off the tape at any time, if they wanted information to be "off the record." Few availed themselves of this opportunity, however. Protocol was followed with respect to Human Subjects Review, and all individuals were apprised of the purpose of the study and informed that their real names would not be used. Almost without exception, interviewees wanted to tell their stories—they felt that they had something to say and that nobody was listening. They ached to share their frustration at the lack of work, to register their disgust at the ways in which they were treated by the welfare office ("downtown"), and to let us, and all the world, know their fears for their children in the midst of a drug economy that seemed to spare no one and, to some, an equally relentless police force. And we were there, promising to tell their story—assuring them we would write *The Unknown City* so that readers would hear the analyses of the poor and working classes at the close of the century.

Upon completing the individual interviews, all data were transcribed (put into hard copy) and input into either Hyperqual (Buffalo) or Ethnograph (Jersey City), computer-based analytic programs for qualitative data. Using traditional qualitative analysis techniques (Bogdan & Taylor, 1975; Bogdan

& Biklen, 1982; Goetz & LeCompte, 1984), we read through over a quarter of the transcripts (across all racial, ethnic, and gender groupings) and established *coding categories*—labels through which the data could be chunked up and analyzed. These empirically developed coding categories were added to our preestablished, theoretically driven codes, ultimately numbering 184 categories, and ranging from "Physical abuse" to "Where from," "Family when growing up," "Childhood fears," "Children," "What community means," and so forth. In line with qualitative research, most categories stem from the data themselves, as filtered, of course, through the investigators' eyes. In other words, few coding categories are predetermined by the investigator; the data have to "speak" to this category in order for it to be set up as one. Interrater reliability scores of at least .80 were established between raters for each code. Each category was assigned a shorter code ("Viol" for "Violence," for example) so that the coding itself was less cumbersome. We then took the code sheet and coded each interview, marking codes on the hard copy. Coding is done in such a way that interview segments can be double coded or even triple coded; that is, one interview segment can be coded as "Church" and "Hard times" and also "Father" at one and the same time. After coding on the hard copy, the transcripts, which had been input into the respective programs, were coded on the screen. We found the qualitative analysis packages useful in this regard, although any word processing program can be set up to do the same, at less cost.

The qualitative analysis programs were terrific as a filing system, but the actual analysis was done by us, using the sorted interview segments as the basis for our analysis. Once all data were coded on screen, print files were established, and data were printed out by our gender and racial categories; these printouts were filed in manila file folders by category. For example, a folder was set up entitled "Current Employment, White Male," into which all utterances by white men related to current work were placed. A similar file on current employment was set up across all demographic groups, so that ultimately statements about work by white females could be compared with those by white males or black women or other groups.

Once the data were all printed out and placed in appropriately labeled manila file folders, our analysis could begin. We read and reread all the full narratives as well as all somewhat decontextualized folders of data snippets, ultimately coming to conclusions about the broader themes that swirled through these stories. As noted throughout *The Unknown City* (Fine & Weis, 1998), the themes which circulated in each community were very different, thus leading to the chapters that we constructed. The preceding chapter, "Cops, Crime, and Violence," derived from a close textual analysis of data coded as "Violence." From a single code, we fanned out into a race, gender, and ethnicity analysis with serious policy implications. In this regard, it was noteworthy that no white male talked about domestic violence, whereas 92 percent of white females did. Since these men and women came from exactly the same communities (churches, schools, and so forth), this led to some of our theorizing as to the silence about this subject in this particular community (Weis, Fine, Proweller, Bertram, & Marusza, 1998).

We must also point out that in qualitative research the coding categories are constituted of, but not necessarily identical to, the themes which constitute later writing. Coding categories are numerous (in our case, 184) and serve as a way of chunking up data so that they can be looked at; it is impossible to analyze systematically thousands of pages of field notes or interview transcripts without coding. Once all data are examined in this way, the categories are recombined by the investigators in order to produce the written research product. Setting up coding categories and subsequent coding are extremely tedious processes, ones which must be done exceedingly carefully. We and our graduate students engaged painstakingly in these processes, over many months time. Coding categories and, later on, themes are not established at the whim of an investigator.

After conducting individual interviews, we conducted focus-group interviews, interviews in which two to seven people met with us at one time in order to probe further issues that came out earlier (Morgan, 1988). In Buffalo, focus groups were conducted in an early childhood center with five African American women; in a Catholic Church with four white women; in an African American church with four black men; and in a Catholic church with three white men. (The overwhelming number of poor and working-class whites in Buffalo are Catholic.) With only two exceptions, all individuals who participated with us in the focus groups had participated in individual interviews as well. In Jersey City, focus groups were conducted with young Latino mothers; white male civil servants; African American, Latino, and white women on public assistance; an African American parenting group; and a group of church-based African American men.

Data from the focus groups were coded similarly to those gathered in individual interviews, although different coding schemes were set up. Questions in focus groups were designed to extend topics which came out as important within gendered and raced communities. Thus the questions posed in each of the focus groups were very different. Groups met over a range of times, from groups with one long substantive meeting to those that sustained themselves over a two-month period and one, the African American men's group in Buffalo, that met again a year later.

We found that group interviews tended to be far more hopeful than individual interviews as we sat with interviewees through many a tearful individual session. While tears certainly flowed in the groups, other members of the group supported and jumped in to tell the tearful person how they had handled particular situations (either with men, children, welfare, or a job). The individual is not left so emotionally spent in a group interview, as participants share their experiences, faith, and hope. While we try to do this in the individual setting, the ambiance of the group is more hopeful. In both sets of interviews, we had information available on activist organizations, support groups, and therapists who worked on a sliding financial scale and would be available and willing to talk with our interviewees. We provided agency names to the interviewees if we felt that it would be useful. Ultimately, however, the decision to call these agencies had to be their own.

The process of analyzing the data took over a year, and then we began to write. Writing was truly collaborative in that we and a number of graduate students circulated papers back and forth (between five and ten drafts per chapter) before producing final essays. Although one of us always took the lead on a chapter, the writing reflects collaborative work at its best, drawing upon all our strengths as we construct essays which set the voices of the poor and working classes of a generation potentially at the center of the policy debates rather than at the margins, where they are now. As we begin a new century, it is important that those historically disenfranchised be heard. It is our hope that policy makers will take their stories seriously; our future as a nation depends on it.

CHAPTER 3

QUALITATIVE RESEARCH, REPRESENTATIONS, AND SOCIAL RESPONSIBILITIES

with Susan Weseen and Mun Wong

I grew up in a world in which talking about somebody's mama was a way of life, an everyday occurrence. For all of us, boys and girls, it was a kind of game or performance. Whether we called it "capping," "snapping," "ranking," "busting," or simply "the dozens," most of it was ridiculous, surreal humor bearing very little resemblance to reality: "Your mom's so fat she broke the food chain"; "Your mama's skin's so ashy she was a stand-in for Casper the Friendly Ghost"; "Your mama's so dumb she thought ring-around-the-collar was a children's game." More than anything, it was an effort to master the absurd metaphor, an art form intended to entertain rather than to damage. . . .

You would think that as a kid growing up in this world I could handle any insult, or at least be prepared for any slander tossed in the direction of my mom—or, for that matter, my whole family, my friends, or my friends' families. But when I entered college and began reading the newspaper, monographs, and textbooks on a regular basis, I realized that many academics, journalists, policymakers, and politicians had taken the "dozens" to another level. In all my years of playing the dozens, I have rarely heard vitriol as vicious as the words spouted by Riverside (California) county welfare director Lawrence Townsend: "Every time I see a bag lady on the street, I wonder, 'Was that an A.F.D.C. mother who hit the menopause wall—who can no longer reproduce and get money to support herself?'" I have had kids tell me that my hair was so nappy it looked like a thousand Africans giving the Black Power salute, but never has anyone said to my face that my whole family—especially my mama—was a "tangle of pathology." Senator Daniel Patrick Moynihan has been saying it since 1965 and, like the one about your mama tying a mattress to her back and offering "roadside service," Moynihan's "snap" has been repeated by legions of analysts and politicians, including Dinesh D'Souza, the boy wonder of the far Right. (Kelly, 1997, pp. 1–2)

In this chapter, we work through the decisions we made about how to represent the consequences of poverty on the lives of poor and working-class men and women in times of punishing, surveilling, and scrutiny by the state. We have discussed some of these issues—alternately called ethics, dilemmas, or simply research—with friends and colleagues. Some think we make "much ado about nothing." Others are relieved that we are "saying aloud" this next generation of troubles. Many wish we would continue to hide under the somewhat transparent robe of even qualitative research. And yet we are compelled to try to move a public conversation about researchers and responsibilities toward a sense of research for social justice.

Because we write between poor communities and social policy and because we seek to be taken seriously by both audiences, we know it is essential to think through the power, obligations, and responsibilities of social research. Entering the contemporary montage of perverse representations of poor and working-class men and women, especially people of color, we write with and for community organizers, policy makers, local activists, the public, and graduate students.

This chapter represents a concrete analysis—an update, perhaps—of what Michelle Fine (1994) has called "working the hyphen."

> Much of qualitative research has reproduced, if contradiction-filled, a colonizing discourse of the "Other." This essay is an attempt to review how qualitative research projects have *Othered* and to examine an emergent set of activist and/or postmodern texts that interrupt *Othering*. First, I examine the hyphen at which Self-Other join in the politics of everyday life, that is, the hyphen that both separates and merges personal identities with our inventions of Others. I then take up how qualitative researchers work this hyphen . . . through a messy series of questions about methods, ethics, and epistemologies as we rethink how researchers have spoken "of" and "for" Others while occluding ourselves and our own investments, burying the contradictions that percolate at the Self-Other hyphen. (p. 70)

We seek not necessarily to engage in simple reflexivity about how our many selves (Jewish, Asian, Canadian, woman, man, straight, gay) coproduce the empirical materials on which we report, although clearly that is an important piece of work (see Ayala et al., 1998). Instead, we gather here a set of self-reflective points of critical consciousness around the questions of how to represent responsibility—that is, transform public consciousness and "common sense" about the poor and working classes, write in ways that attach lives to racial structures and economies, and construct stories and analyses that interrupt and reframe the victim-blaming mantras of the 1990s.

Writing against the grain, we thought it useful to speak aloud about the politics and scholarship of decisions we have made.

FLEXING OUR REFLEXIVITIES

In the social sciences, both historically and presently, the relationship be-tween researcher and subject has been "obscured in social science texts, protecting privilege, securing distance, and laminating the contradictions" (Fine, 1994, p. 72). There has long been a tendency to view the self of the social science observer as a potential contaminant, something to be sepa-rated out, neutralized, minimized, standardized, and controlled. This bracketing of the researcher's world is evident in social science's histori-cally dominant literary style (Madigan, Johnson, & Linton, 1995) that is predicated on a "clarion renunciation" of the subjective or personal aspects of experience (Morawski & Bayer, 1995), particularly those of researchers. As Ruth Behar (1993) explains, "We ask for revelations from others, but we reveal little or nothing of ourselves; we make others vulnerable, but we ourselves remain invulnerable" (p. 273). Our informants are then left carrying the burden of representations, as we hide behind the alleged cloak of neutrality.

Although it may be true that researchers are never absent from our texts, the problem of just how to "write the self [and, we would add, write our political reflexivities] into the text" (Billig, 1994, p. 326) remains. Simply briefly inserting autobiographical or personal information often serves to establish and assert the researcher's authority, ultimately producing texts "from which the self has been sanitized" (Okely, 1992, p. 5). But flooding the text with ruminations on researchers' subjectivities also has the poten-tial to silence participants, or "subjects" (Lal, 1996).

It should also be pointed out that a call for the inclusion of subjective experience of the researcher into what has traditionally been conceived of as subject matter bears different implications for differently situated re-searchers. In the hands of relatively privileged researchers studying those whose experiences have been marginalized, the reflexive mode's poten-tial to silence subjects is of particular concern. It is easy for reflexivity to slip into what Patricia Clough (1992) has called a "compulsive extrover-sion of inferiority" (p. 63). In the words of Renato Rosaldo (1989), "If classic ethnography's vice was the slippage from the ideal of detachment to actual indifference, that of present-day reflexivity is the tendency for the self-absorbed Self to lose sight altogether of the culturally different Other" (p. 7). Yet from an entirely different and overlapping perspective, some critical race theorists (e.g., Ladner, 1971; Lawrence, 1995; Matsuda, 1995) have suggested that, for people of color whose stories have not been told, "the assertion of our subjective presence as creators and interpreters of text are political acts" (Lawrence, 1995, p. 349). According to Donna Haraway (1991), "Vision is always a question of the power to see—and perhaps of the violence implicit in our visualizing practices" (p. 192); who is afforded—or appropriates—this power to see and speak about what is seen as well as what is hidden from scrutiny is a question that is at the heart of our examinations of our social responsibilities to write and "re-present" in a time of ideological assault on the poor. Thus we seek to narrate a form of reflexivity in our concerns with representation and responsibilities in these very mean times.

THE TEXTUAL SUBJECT

In the remainder of this chapter, we reflect on the materials drawn for a book written by Michelle Fine and Lois Weis about poor and working-class city dwellers at the end of the twentieth century. In this work, *The Unknown City* (1998), we (Fine and Weis) have centered the voices, politics, disappointments, and hopes of young urban adults of the poor and working classes. These men and women—African American, white, and Latino—render oral histories of their struggles, victories, and passions, detailing lives filled with work—and its absence—schooling, family life, spirituality, sexuality, violence on the streets and in their homes, and social movements that seem no longer vibrant. Our analyses suggest that these young adults, men and women, constitute an unknown, unheard-from, and negatively represented constituency of our American democracy. Between the ages of 23 and 35, with neither the resources nor the sense of entitlement typically narrated by members of Generation X, they have been displayed and dissected in the media as the *cause* of national problems. Depicted as being the reason for the rise in urban crime, they are cast as if they embody the necessity for welfare reform, as if they sit at the heart of moral decay. While much of contemporary social policy is designed to "fix" them, our investigation reveals that they have much to say back to policy makers and the rest of America.

The late 1990s witnessed a flood of books written about and sometimes despite those who have been grouped together as the poor and working classes. But this group, particularly the young, are fundamentally unknown, at once quite visible as "moral spectacle" (Roman, 1997) and yet "fundamentally invisible" (A. J. Franklin, personal communication, October 14, 1997). As our nation walks away from their needs, desires, strengths, and yearnings, it abandons a generation. Millions of poor and working-class children continue to grow up amidst the wreckage of global corporate restructuring, in the shadows of once bustling urban factories, a reinvigorated U.S. nationalism and racism, and a wholesale depletion of the public safety net, and, at the same time, witness increasing violence in their communities and often in their homes. And mostly, they blame themselves and each other. The state retreat from the social good and the corporate flight from urban centers, the north, and the U.S.A. are shockingly absent as blame is doled out. As calls to reverse civil rights, Affirmative Action, welfare, and immigration policies gain momentum, it is noteworthy that the voices of the men and women in the poor and working classes are never heard.

The Unknown City reveals not only common pains within the poor and working classes but also a deeply fractured urban America in the late twentieth century. In spite of legislation and social politics designed to lessen inequality and promote social cohesion in the 1960s, at the turn of the century, the nation stands deeply divided along racial, ethnic, social-class, and gender lines. Our goals in the book, then, were to examine the commonalities and fractured nature of American society, focusing on what we call "communities of difference," as low-income people settle for crumbs in one of the richest nations of the world. We sought, further, to place these voices at the center of national debates about social policy rather than at the margin, where they currently stand. This chapter consciously reflects back on the work of writing this book: our headaches and struggles, as we entered the battle of representations happening on, about, and despite, but rarely with, poor and working-class urban dwellers at the end of the twentieth century. Amidst economic dislocation and a contracted public sphere we seek to re-present men and women navigating lives of joy and disappointment, anger and laughter, despair and prayer.

Much as we sought to escape the narrow confines of demographic, essentialist categories, what we heard from both Jersey City and Buffalo tended to bring us back to these categories. That is, much as we all know, read, teach, and write about race, class, and gender as social constructions (see Fine, Powell, Weis, & Wong, 1997), loaded with power and complexity, always in quotation marks, when we listened to the taped interviews with African American men living in Jersey City or Buffalo, they were strikingly different from those of white men, or Latinas, or African American women. Indeed, both the very distinct material bases and cumulative historic circumstances of each of these groups, and the enormous variety *within* categories, demanded intellectual and political respect. So we tell the "big story" of people living in poverty as well as the particular stories narrated through gender, race, and ethnicity. Thus, we write with and through poststructural understandings of identity and possibility, ever returning to "common" material bases (the economy, state, and the body) as we move through the nuances of "differences."

ON FRAMING THE WORK

On Community

Perhaps our most vexing theoretical dilemma swirled around the question, "So, what constitutes a community?" How do we write about real estate, land-bounded communities, like Buffalo or Jersey City, geographically valid, zip code varied, "real" spaces in which we nevertheless found so little in the way of psychologically or socially shared biographies or visions?

We recognized from our theoretical interests, confirmed by the narratives we collected, that profound fractures, as well as variation, cut through life within these communities. Simple demographic nuances, by race/ethnicity, gender, class, generation, and sexuality, marked dramatic distinctions in experience. Within local neighborhoods or racial/ethnic groups, gender, sexuality, and generational divisions boldly sever what may appear to be, at first glance, internal continuities (see West, 1993). For instance, within the presumably "same" part of Jersey City, African Americans refer to local police practices with stories of harassment and fear while whites are far more likely to complain about a rise in crime and brag about a brother-in-law who is a cop (see Chapter 1). While Jersey City whites described the "good old days" of economic security and pined for the day when they would be moving to Bayonne, African Americans from the same block harbored few wistful memories of "good old days" and routinely avoid "getting stopped at red lights" in Bayonne, lest their stay be extended beyond what they expected.

At historic moments of job security and economic hard times, the presumed harmony of poor and working-class communities grows ravaged by further interior splits, finger-pointing, blame, and suspicion. Coalitions are few, even if *moments* of interdependence-for-survival are frequent. Within homes, differences and conflicts explode, cross-gender and cross-generation. A full sense of community is fictional and fragile, ever vulnerable to external threats and internal fissures. While there is a class-based story to be told, a sense of class-based coherence prevails only if our methods fail to interrogate differences by race/ethnicity, gender, and sexuality. And yet, at the same time, commonalities *across* cities—by demography and biography—were all the more striking.

We could, therefore, write about life within these two urban communities, Jersey City and Buffalo, as though the notion of community were unproblematic, a geographic space of shared experience. Or we could, with equal ease and discomfort, present a book about African American men and women, white men and women, and Latinos and Latinas as though each group experiences a social world totally insulated from that of others. Although some of our data press toward the latter, our theoretical and political inclinations make us look toward the former, searching for common ground, shared languages, and parallel experiences. Our text tries to speak, at once, in these two dialects, to issues of the common and the specific, without diluting either. We decided to offer two chapter forms in *The Unknown City*: one which privileges the unique experiences of groups—for example, African American men—and another which explores the ways in which poor and working-class people travel over similar terrain—schooling, motherhood, or crime—in their lives. Scripting a story in which we float a semifictional portrait of each community, we layered over an analytic matrix of differences within. For our analysis—within and between cities—we delicately move between coherence and difference, fixed boundaries and porous borders, neighborhoods of shared values and homes of contentious interpretations.

On "Race"

Robin Kelly (1997) describes his latest book as "a defense of black people's humanity and a condemnation of scholars and policymakers for their inability to see complexity" (p. 4). Some academics have addressed this complexity: Henry Louis Gates (1985) has written beautifully about "race," always using quotes; Michael Dyson (1993) argues against narrow nationalistic or essentialist definitions for either skin color or language; Kimberlé Crenshaw (1989) forces us to theorize at the intersections of race and gender; Stuart Hall (1981) narrates the contextual instability of racial identities, as do Michael Omi and Howard Winant (1986). Like these theorists, our informants use, employ, or conceive of race as both a floating, unstable fiction and also a fundamental, unerasable aspect of biography and social experience. Indeed, some of our informants, like the one below, suggest that "race" constitutes inherently undefinable territory, offering narratives not so much of denial as complexity.

Mun: Your dad?

Luisa: Yes, my dad was the craziest Puerto Rican you had ever seen in the '70s. Oh my Lord.

Mun: What is your mom's background?

Luisa: Mom, Mom was raised Catholic, but in my mother's day, when an Irish and German woman went with a Chinese guy, in those days that was like, oh no, no that cannot happen. My grandfather had to drop his whole family for my grandmother, so they could be together. Everybody disowned him in this family.

Mun: Because he married a . . .

Luisa: Yeah, he married my grandmother.

Mun: What about your mom's side?

Luisa: That is my mom's side.

Mun: What about your grandfather's side?

Luisa: My grandfather, he was in Vietnam, World War II, oh, I forgot the name. It was a very big war, that I know.

Mun: Korean War?

Luisa: Yeah, something like that, I just can't remember what it was. Yeah, he had honors and everything my mother told me.

Mun: So you looked very different?

Luisa: Yeah, I'm a mixture.

Mun: You have Chinese blood?

Luisa: Right. I got Irish and German, I got Puerto Rican and Italian, I have a lot. I'm a mixed breed.

Mun: I was wondering. The first time I saw you I thought you were from the Middle East.

Luisa: From the Middle East?

Mun: Yeah.

Luisa: Oh, golly gee, no. I'm, like, really mixed. I'm like everything. I got all these different personalities that just come out all the time. I swear to God. No lie. No lie.

When we began our interviews in Jersey City and Buffalo, we also were taken by poststructural thinking on questions of "race." With Stuart Hall (1997) particularly in mind, willing to acknowledge the artificiality, the performances, and, indeed, the racist roots of the notion of race (1/32 drop of blood, and so forth), we constructed an interview protocol that generously invited our informants to "play" with "race" as we had. So we asked, in many clever ways, for them to describe time- and context-specific racial identifications—when they fill out census forms, walk through supermarkets, when alone or among friends. Informants of color tried to be polite and follow us in our play, but by hour three grew exasperated with these questions. White interviewees either thought we were calling them racist or avoided identifying as white, instead speaking about being Irish, Italian, or human. Needless to say, the playfulness of the questions did not work.

Many argued that race *should not* make much of a difference.[1] And we, too, wanted to write that book, not out of liberal foolishness but from profound political commitments to class, race, and gender analyses and to "what *should* be." And yet, as we listened to our data, the life stories, as narrated, were so thoroughly drenched in racializing discourse that readers could not help but know even an anonymous informant's racial group once they read the transcript. Personal stories of violence and family structure, narrative style, one's history with money, willingness to trash (publicly) violent men and marriages, access to material resources, relations with kin and the state, descriptions of interactions with the police were all talked through "race."

"Race" is a place in which poststructuralism and lived realities need to talk. "Race" is a social construction, indeed. But "race" in a racist society bears profound consequence for daily life, identity, social movements, and the ways in which most groups *other*. But how we write about "race" to a deeply race-bound audience worries us. Do we take the category for granted, as if unproblematic? By so doing, we (re)inscribe its fixed and essentialist positionality. Do we instead problematize it theoretically, knowing full well its full-bodied impact on daily life? Yes, "race" *is* a social construction, but it is so deeply confounded with racism that it bears enormous power in and seepage into lives and communities. To the informants with whom we spoke, "race" does exist—it saturates every pore of their lives.

How can we destabilize the notion theoretically, at one and the same time as we recognize the lived presence of "race"?

To give a trivial, but telling, example, here is a problem that may appear at face value to be a sampling problem incidentally related to "race." We struggled in both cities to find "equally poor" and "equally working-class" African American, Latino, and white young adults so that comparisons by race/ethnicity would not be confounded by class. Guess what? The world is lousy with confounds. While we did find poor and working-class whites, the spread and depth of their poverty was nowhere near as severe as in the African American sample. Our ambitious search for sampling comparability, in spite of our meticulous combing of raced neighborhoods, lost hands down to the profound lived realities of multigenerational poverty disproportionately affecting poor and working-class families of color (Oliver & Shapiro, 1995). What may appear to be a methodological problem has been revealed as constitutive of the very fabric of society. Neither problematizing nor (re)inscribing "race" in our writing will help us, as a society, to confront the very real costs and privileges of racial categorization.

INFORM(ING) AND CONSENT: WHO'S INFORMED AND WHO'S CONSENTING?

With frame more or less clear, we move to the interviews. At this point, we struggle through the ethics of constructing narratives with poor men and women, each paid $40 for an interview. So, we ask, what is consent? And for whom? Mun Wong confronted this dilemma often. The informed consent form for our interviews states:

> We are conducting interviews with young adults on their perceptions of high school experiences and since. We are particularly interested in discussing concerns, attitudes, and aspirations (then and now) developed during your years in high school. . . . I, [respondent's name], agree to participate in this study on the urban experiences of young adults growing up in Jersey City (Buffalo) during the 1980s and 1990s. The interviews will be audiotaped, transcribed, and written up in a book. No names will be attached to the interviews.

The consent form sits at the contradictory base of the institutionalization of research. Although the aim of informed consent is presumably to protect respondents, informing them of the possibility of harm in advance, and inviting them to withdraw if they so desire, it also effectively releases the institution or funding agency from any liability and gives control of the research process to the researcher. Commenting on this standard formulaic piece of the research process, Brinton Lykes (1989) writes, "Reflecting on my experiences with the [informed consent] form revealed the complexity of both my role as researcher/activist and the constraints on developing collaboration between subjects in a context of real power imbalances" (p. 177). She continues:

> The informed consent form, which I introduced as a mechanism for "protecting the subjects" of the research project, was instead a barrier and forced me to confront the chasm between the needs and demands of research conducted within the boundaries of the university and the systems of trust and mistrust and of sharing and withholding that were already a part of this collaboration. (p. 178)

In our work, we have come to understand how the introduction of an informed consent form requires analysis as much as that which is routinely and easily considered as data, such as the narratives of our participants. The (apparent) rapport that Mun had with respondents seemed to unravel whenever he handed out the consent form. Many of them asked him, "What is this for?" He was always embarrassed when an explanation was required, in many cases simply mumbling an explanation. In some cases, contrary to official research protocol, he presented the consent form in the second part of the interview. Even so, many women simply signed the form as just another procedural matter, without reading the entire document. Their (apparent) nonchalance probably reflected their general attitude toward procedural matters. These respondents—women on welfare—are constantly required to read bureaucratic forms, which are convoluted and technical, and are told to sign off others' responsibilities, while signing onto their own.

The informed consent form forced us to confront and contend with the explicitly differential relationships between the respondents and ourselves, becoming a crude tool—a conscience—to remind us of our accountability and position. Stripping us of our illusions of friendship and reciprocity, it made "working the hyphen" even more difficult. No matter how hard Mun tried to downplay "differences" and find a common ground from which to proceed, our participants' responses to the informed consent form reminded us to dispel any artificial attempts at displacing differences (Borland, 1991).

Judith Stacey (1991) has argued that (feminist) ethnography depends upon human relationships, engagement and attachment, with the research process potentially placing research subjects at grave risk of manipulation and betrayal.

> Situations of inauthenticity, dissimilitude, and potential, perhaps inevitable, betrayal situations are inherent in fieldwork research. For no matter how welcome, even enjoyable, the field worker's presence may appear to locals, social work often represents an intrusion and intervention into a system of relationships, a system of relationships that the researcher is far freer than the researched to leave. The inequality and potential treacherousness of this relationship is inescapable. (p. 113)

Dorcy came up to Mun after he finished his interview with Regina. She told him that she also wanted to be part of the study, and he told her that he would get to her when he completed the interviews with Melissa and Diane. So for the next three weeks or so, whenever Mun ran into her, she would ask, "When is my turn?" Mun would always give his typical reply to women who kept requesting an interview, "You are next, next week, okay?" "You better make sure," Dorcy laughed. Her repeated, though friendly, gestures, along with her gigglish laughs and timid smiles were constant reminders: "I thought you said it was my turn."

At the beginning of their first interview, they sat facing each other across a table. Mun started off with his script: "Thanks for doing this. As you know, I am interviewing women about their experiences on welfare but also try to get a picture of their lives. This is a consent form, and you may want to read it first. If you agree to abide by whatever is written there, please sign it. And I am going to tape-record this. Also, if you do not feel comfortable with whatever, just say you are going to skip it, okay?" She signed the form, and the taped interview began.

Mun: How was your family ... when you were growing up?
Dorcy: Oh, I had ... I had a good growing ... growing ... I had it good. My mother, my father. My father died when I was twelve. So, he was ... he was always there for us, ya know. My mother, she's good. She's a strong woman. She love us and she take care of us ... things we need ... and she help us out a lot ... yeah.
Mun: How many brothers and sisters do you have?
Dorcy: Excuse me?

Mun: Brothers and sisters?

Dorcy: Oh ... um ... three sisters, I make three sisters, and five brothers.
      I have ... one of my brother died of AIDS, in '91 ... of November
      ... he died of AIDS.

Mun: What number are you?

Dorcy: I'm 25.

Mun: I mean, number in the family.

Dorcy: Oh, I'm ... I'm in the middle.

Mun: [laughs]

Dorcy: [laughs] ... I'm the middle ... middle child.

Mun: Is it good?

Dorcy: It's good.

Mun: I mean ... what ...

Dorcy: It has its ups and downs, but it's good.

Mun: What do you mean?

Dorcy: Huh?

Mun: Ups and downs?

Dorcy: Because like, the oldest get things first and the baby get ... more
      ... the most things before the middle child will get. [And the inter-
      view continued.]

At first glance, this extract does not seem different from the other women. But if one looks more closely—and especially if one listens to the tape—her hesitations, monosyllabic answers, and reluctance to speak up become noticeable. This is in sharp contrast to her speech outside of the interview process, as well as that of most of the other women interviewed. At the end of the day, Mun recorded this short memo in his fieldnotes.

> Interviewed Dorcy today. She has been urging me for the past two weeks to interview her. And when I was talking to her today, she was giving me monosyllabic answers and speaking in such a soft tone that I could hardly make out a word she was speaking. She was driving me nuts with her inarticulations and "I don't know" ... she refuses to elaborate her stories and discuss about her life. I don't know why I chose her ... I should have stuck to my initial choice of either Mary or Annie.

Thinking that their bantering and gestures were a process in developing a friendship, he felt a sense of betrayal, and now he wondered whether her friendliness had been a kind of staged performance designed to win his confidence.

Judith Stacey (1991) contends that in our fieldwork, the respondents' lives, loves, and tragedies that fieldwork informants share with a researcher are ultimately data—"grist for the ethnographic mill, a mill that has a truly grinding power" (p. 113). When the women are informed and they consent, does this mean that their stories (and aspects of their lives they choose—or feel compelled—to share) no longer belong to them? Does Mun, for example, inform the welfare agency of their problems with particular staff members? Does he interrupt or simply collect narration of the women's racial antagonisms, between and among groups? What about the time when Rosita told him in the corridor that she saw her batterer ex-boyfriend walking with the program administrator, Deborah, the person who generously opened the program for his research? How best to respond to the information presented in one of the focus groups that Rosita had been sexually harassed by one of the instructors? Mun found himself working between an organization that was generous enough to allow us access, and the allegiance and hard-earned trust from respondents. In many of these cases, he was the opportunistic "fly on the wall," recording observations without seeming to become entangled in these ethical conundrums (Roman, 1993). But as Stacey has noted, ethnographic method is more likely to leave subjects exposed to exploitation: the greater the intimacy, according to Stacey, the greater is the danger. And yet, contrary to this view, many of the women and men we interviewed both recognized and delightfully exploited the power inequalities in the interview process. They recognized that we could take their stories, their concerns, and their worries to audiences, policy-makers, and the public in ways that they themselves could not. They (and we) knew that we traded on class and race privilege to get a counter-narrative out. And so they consented. They were both informed and informing.

THEN, THE STORIES

As we just suggested, worries over consent are closely related to worries about "bad stories" we collected.

Mun: Do you feel that your word is not trusted, that you need someone else to say, you need a lawyer or psychiatrist to say everything is okay now?

Tara: Because of DYFS [Division for Youth and Family Services], yes.

Mun: But you can't have . . .

Tara: They won't, yeah. They won't just take you for your word, no. You need to have . . .

Mun: You need to have somebody else say that for you?

Tara: Yes. DYFS, yes.

Mun: How would DYFS treat your kids, though?

Tara: Because when you get child, they say I put their life in danger, because I did, but I was . . . I was in jail, I was in the psychiatric ward. They had to do the best interest for the children, I couldn't take care of them at the time.

Mun: Oh, so DYFS took your kids?

Tara: Yeah, so DYFS gave them to their father. I'm in court now.

Mun: At least it's not foster care, though.

Tara: That's what I said. They're with family. They might hate it there, they can't stand it. My kids say that they're treated worse.

Mun: They hate their father?

Tara: No, they don't hate their father, they hate their grandmother, they hate the mother-in-law, they hate their grandmother. They don't like their grandmother.

Mun: His mother?

Tara: Yeah, they don't like their aunts, their uncles.

Mun: They are a lot of Puerto Ricans?

Tara: They're all Puerto Ricans, but my kids were always like the outcasts because they didn't like me, so my kids, my kids, I mean, George was seven years old, seven years of George's life, George had to have seen his grandmother six times. Nicole, in the three years of her life, never seen them. You know, my kids got dumped into a family that they know nothing about.

What does it mean to uncover some of what we have uncovered? How do we handle "hot" information, especially in times when poor and working-class women and men are being demonized by the Right and by Congress? How do we connect theoretically, empirically, and politically troubling social/familial patterns with macrostructural shifts when our informants *expressly do not*—or even refuse—to make the connections?

The hegemony of autonomous individualism forces a self-conscious, imposed theorizing (by us) of especially bad stories, well beyond the perspectives expressed by most of our informants. So, for instance, what do we do with information about the ways in which women on welfare virtually have to become welfare cheats in order to survive: "Sure he comes once a month and gives me some money. I may have to take a beating, but the kids need the money" (Edin & Lein, 1997)? A few use more drugs than we wished to know; most are wonderful parents, but some underattend to their children well beyond neglect. These are the dramatic consequences, and perhaps also the facilitators, of hard economic times. To ignore the information is to deny the effects of poverty, racism, and abuse. To report these stories is to risk their more-than-likely misuse, in view of the fact that we were not also studying and attending to elite tax evasion, elite use of drugs, and elite neglect of children.

In a moment in history when there are few audiences willing to reflect on the complex social roots of community and domestic violence, the economic impossibilities of sole reliance on welfare, or even the willingness to appreciate the complexity, love, hope, and pain that fills the poor and working class—how do we put out for display the voyeuristic dirty laundry that litters our transcripts? Historian Daryl Michael Scott (1997), in his provocative book, *Contempt and Pity*, places in historical perspective the perverse historic use of the "damaged black psyche" by both the Left and the Right today. To what extent do we contribute to this perverse legacy? Is it better if white poor and working classes are also portrayed as "damaged"? At the same time, is it not unethical to romanticize, and thereby deny, the devastating impact of the current and historic assault on poor and working-class families launched through the state, the economy, neighbors, and sometimes kin? We are left, then, with two questions. First, must we, social scientists, document damage in order to justify claims about oppression and injustice? And, second, what is the role of the public intellectual in rewriting, that is, interrupting the "common sense" script of *their* damage (and, of course, *our* wholeness) and offering up, instead, a discourse of national damage, outrage, and demands for justice?

With interviews over, we continue to struggle with how to best represent the stories that may do more harm than good, depending on who consumes or exploits them: stories that reveal the adult consequences of child physical and sexual abuse; stories that suggest it is almost impossible to live exclusively on welfare payments, encouraging many to lie about their incomes so that they self-define as "welfare cheats"; stories in which white respondents, in particular, portray people of color in gross and dehumanizing ways; data on the depth of violence in women's lives, across race/

ethnicity. To what extent are we responsible to list "Warning! Misuse of data can be hazardous to our collective national health"?

There are some academics writing about such concerns (Cross, 1991; hooks, 1992; Lather, 1986), but few who write about and work with activists to reimagine social research for social justice (for such wonderful work, see Lykes, 1989; Saegert, 1997; Austin, 1992). It is up to all of us to figure out how to say what needs to be said without jeopardizing individuals and feeding perverse social representations (McCarthy, Rodriguez, Meecham, David, Wilson-Brown, Godina, Supryia, & Buendia, 1997).

As with bad stories, we worried about our voyeuristic search for "good stories." While engaged in interviewing, the research assistants would gather informally and share stories. We talked about respondents not showing up for their interviews, the lives of interviewees, "funny things that happened along the way," our pain, and our early understanding of the material. The words and phrases thrown around included: "interesting," "boring," "nothing out of the ordinary," "you should have heard this," and "this one has great stories." But just what did we mean by "great stories?"

Great stories can be read as allegories, which shed light both on the level of content and the implications of that content. Allegory, as James Clifford (1986) reminds us,

> denotes a practice in which a narrative fiction continuously refers to another pattern of ideas or events. It is a representation that represents itself—[It is] a story [that] has a propensity to generate another story in the mind of its reader (or hearer), to repeat and displace some prior story. . . . A recognition of allegory emphasizes the fact that realistic portraits, to the extent that they are "convincing" or "rich," are extended metaphors, patterns of associations that point to coherent (theoretical, esthetic, moral) additional meanings. . . . Allegory draws attention to the narrative character of cultural representations, to the stories built into the representational process itself. (pp. 99–100)

We worry that what appear to be great stories might, however, feed our collective misunderstandings and renderings of the poor. Like experimenters who are inevitably inflicted with and inflicting "experimenter's bias," qualitative researchers carry misconceptions and "alluring fictions" (Clifford, 1986) of the subject. We enter the scene looking for stories and may, at times, "unintentionally behav[e] in such a way as to make the prophesied event more likely to occur" (Suls & Rosnow, 1988, p. 168). By looking for great stories, we potentially walk into the field with constructions of the "other," however benevolent or benign they seem, feeding the politics of representation and becoming part of the negative figuration of poor women and men.

For us, the fundamental good story is not simply one laced with social problems such as homelessness, welfare, and sexual harassment—a victim who is harassed, battered, and overwhelmed by problems. In retrospect, we admit that we also searched for agents who "resisted," enacting the role of the critic of the state and/or economic relations. As Mun's interviews with women on welfare proceeded, he always hoped that they would be perfect critics, able to pierce the veil of structured and state hypocrisy. It is interesting to note that so many hegemonic and victim-blaming positions were narrated by these profoundly oppressed men and women; judgments about "others" often resonated with a broad cultural discourse of holding victims of poverty, racism, and sexual violence accountable for their woes. In many of our interviews, poor women on welfare blamed other women, labeling them as "welfare queens," "neglectful mothers," and "insensitive bureaucrats." Our own romanticized images of the resister—one who desires to speak out against injustice and act with a collective—turned on us.

Once we collect great (and not so great) stories from our respondents, the next difficult stage is the interpretation, representation, and analysis of data. We have, at times, consciously and deliberately left out some of these great stories, ones that have the potential to become "bad data" to buttress stereotypes, reaffirm the ideology and rhetoric of the Right, and reinscribe dominant representations. As Hurtado and Stewart (1997) have written, the repetition of certain hurtful and vicious opinions and attitudes will inflict pain on those who are the "victims." In such cases, what is required is "minimal documentation, when views are all-too-familiar and oppressive, while holding ourselves and others to a very high standard of analytic depth when work causes such a high risk of causing suffering in those already the objects of daily racism" (p. 308). And also required, we would add, is a close focus on the mundane.

What happens to the dull details of negotiating daily life in poverty that do not capture our attention in the way that great stories do?

Well, I take . . . I get $424 a month, okay? And I get $270 in food stamps, so I take . . . there's four weeks to a month, so I take . . . I take the $270 and I divide it by four. And that's what I spend on food. It's just me and my daughters. And my oldest don't eat that much and I don't eat . . . I only eat once a day. I only eat dinner. I'm not hungry in the morning and I don't have breakfast. I have a cup of coffee or hot

chocolate. My little one is the one that eats a lot. And whatever I don't
... like I spend $65 a week in food. I go and I buy meat every day and I
buy their breakfast, their lunch, her snacks for school. And whenever I
can ... I work at night ... I work ... if I get a call I go and clean
somebody's house. I do that. Their father gives me money, you know. So
I do whatever I ... you know, whatever it takes, you know? Shovel your
snow ... [laughs] I don't care. You know, to me money's money, as long
as your kids got what they need. But basically their father helps me the
most. You know, he'll come in ... oh, my dad does this, too, and I get
really pissed off at him. He'll come in and he'll start looking through my
cabinets and in my refrigerator, and my closet. "Well, what do you have
here?" And it's like, "I'm fine. Johnny's coming over later." "No! Blah, blah,
blah." And he'll go out and he'll come back with food, and their father's
always coming in looking through the refrigerator, and things like that, you
know? I always ... my kids have food, so that's good, you know? They
never go hungry. You know, I ... I hate to say this, but if I had ... I
mean, if it came to where my kids were gonna go hungry, I'd sell my
body. To hell with that! My kids ain't gonna starve, you know? I'd do
what it takes. I would give two shits. People could ... my friends could
tell me whatever they wanted. I have a ... I have two friends that sell
their bodies for money for their kids. And thank God, I have to knock on
wood, I never had to take a loan, if I had to, I would. If that's what it
took to feed my kids ... I mean, if their father ... a lot of people that
are on welfare have husbands worth shit. They don't care. If they had a
father, but I guess that's, if that's what it took ... I would try every aspect
before doing that. But if that's what it really took to feed my kids, that's
what I would do. I would do whatever it takes to feed and clothe my
kids, you know, and put a roof over their head. I wouldn't care what the
hell it was. I guess that's what I would do, you know?

When we listen to and read narratives, we researchers tend to be drawn
to—in fact, to *code for*—the exotic, the bizarre, the violent. As we reflect on
narratives of poverty, we nevertheless feel obligated to explore meticu-
lously the very tedious and mundane sections of the transcripts; those huge
sections that are not very exciting, the mundane spots, when *they*—the
informants—do what *we*—the researchers—admit that we do: walk their
kids to school, read the newspaper, turn on the television for a break, look
for a doctor they can trust, hope their children are safe on the way home

from school. These mundane rituals of daily living—obviously made much more difficult in the presence of poverty and discrimination, but mundane nonetheless—are typically left out of ethnographic descriptions of life in poverty. They do not make very good reading, and yet these are the stuff of daily life. We recognize how careful we need to be so that we do not construct life narratives spiked only with the hot spots.

Different Methods, Different Stories

Once the interviews are complete, triangulation surfaces as a critical element in the practice of social science: "adding" one layer of data to another to build a confirmatory edifice. In quantitative data analysis, triangulation occurs when multiple items, within the same scale, measure the same construct, or when two different scales join to measure the same construct. In psychological research in particular, and sociological research at times, the tendency is to use qualitative methods to supplement quantitative data.

However, in our work, conducted primarily through narratives but also through surveys on political engagement, we were not looking for a simple coherent synthesis of data or methods. With a firm reliance on multiple methods, we sought to cross over, converse, and tap into the different kinds of data; we searched for the very contradictions between methods that would most powerfully inform policy. We learned what Fine and Weis (1996) have written elsewhere:

> Methods are not passive strategies. They differently produce, reveal, and enable the display of different kinds of identities. To be more specific, if individual interviews produce the most despairing stories, evince the most minimal sense of possibility, present identities of victimization, and voice stances of hopelessness, in focus groups with the same people the despair begins to evaporate, a sense of possibility sneaks through, and identities multiply as informants move from worker to mother, to friend, to lover, to sister, to spiritual healer, to son, to fireman, to once-employed, to welfare recipient. In the context of relative safety, trust, comfort, and counterhegemonic creativity offered by the few free spaces into which we have been invited, a far more textured and less judgmental sense of self is displayed. In these like-minded communities that come together to trade despair and build hope, we see and hear a cacophony of voices filled with spirit, possibility, and a sense of vitality absent in the individual data. (pp. 267–268)

We recognize that different methodologies are likely to illuminate different versions of men's and women's understandings of welfare, jobs, education, and violence. Convergence is unlikely and, perhaps, undesirable. Following a poststructuralist emphasis on contradiction, heterogeneity, and multiplicity, we produced a quilt of stories and a cacophony of voices speaking to each other in dispute, dissonance, support, dialogue, contention, and contradiction. Once women's and men's subjectivities are considered and sought after *as if* multiple, varied, conflicting, and contradictory, then the "data elicited" are self-consciously dependent upon the social locations of participants and the epistemological assumptions of the methods. We join Kum Kum Bhavnani (1993) who demands that multiple methods and a deep commitment to engaging with differences (particularly between researcher and researched) form the core of provocative, politically engaged social science, so that we

> cannot be complicit with dominant representations which reinscribe inequality. It follows from a concern with power and positioning that the researcher must address the micro-politics of the conduct of research and . . . given the partiality of all knowledge, questions of differences must not be suppressed but built into research. (p. 98)

Denzin and Lincoln (1994) suggest,

> Qualitative research is inherently multimethod in focus (Brewer & Hunter, 1989). However, the use of multiple methods, or triangulation, reflects the phenomenon in question. Objective reality can never be captured. Triangulation is not a tool or a strategy of validation, but an alternative to validation (Denzin, 1989a, 1989b, p. 244; Fielding & Fielding, 1986, p. 33; Flick, 1992, p. 194). The combination of multiple methods, empirical materials, perspectives and observers in a single study is best understood, then, as a strategy that adds rigor, breadth and depth to any investigation (see Flick, 1992, p. 1940). (p. 2)

In Whose Voice?

Mark, a white working-class informant, tells us:

> It goes into another subject where blacks, um, I have nothing against blacks. Um, whether you're black, white, you know, yellow, whatever color, whatever race. But I don't like the black movement where, I have

black friends. I talk to them and they agree. You know, they consider
themselves, you know, there's white trash and there's white, and there's
black trash and there's blacks. And the same in any, you know, race. But
as soon as they don't get a job, they right away call, you know, they yell
discrimination.

In whose voice do we write? Well, of course, our own. But we also present
long narratives, colorful and edited, drawn with/from informants. Some of
these narratives, particularly from the sample of working-class and poor
white men contain hostile, sometimes grotesque references to "others"—
people of color, women, black men on the corner. As theorists, we refrain
from the naive belief that these voices should stand on their own or that
voices should (or do) survive without theorizing. However, we also find
ourselves differentially theorizing and contextualizing voices. That is, those
voices that have been historically smothered—for example, voices of
working-class white women, and men and women of color—we typically
present on their own terms, perhaps reluctant to surround them with much
of *our* theory (Weis, Marusza, & Fine, 1998). And yet, when we present the
voices of white men who seem eminently expert at fingering African
American men for all their pain and plight, we theorize boldly, contextualize
wildly, rudely interrupting *them* to re-frame them (Weis & Fine, 1996; Weis,
Proweller, & Centrie, 1997).

Is this an epistemological double standard in need of reform, or is it a
form of narrative affirmative action, creating discursive spaces where few
have been in the past? Aida Hurtado and Abigail Stewart (1997), in a
fascinating essay, "Through the Looking Glass: Implications of Studying
Whiteness for Feminist Methods," argue that feminist scholars should self-
consciously *underplay* (e.g., not quote extensively) hegemonic voices in
our essays and as relentlessly create textual room for counter hegemonic
narratives. While we agree, we also think it is vitally important for us to
analyze, critically, what it is that white men are saying about us, about them,
about economic and social relations. To do this, we interpret their words,
their stories, and their assertions about "others."

This raises what we have come to think of as the "triple representational
problem." We ponder how we present (1) *ourselves* as researchers choreo-
graphing the narratives we have collected; (2) the *narrators*, many of whom
are wonderful social critics, while some, from our perspective, are talented
ventriloquists for a hateful status quo; and (3) the *"others"* who are graphi-
cally bad-mouthed by these narrators, for example, caseworkers blamed for

stinginess and disrespect by women on welfare, African American men who are held responsible for all social evils by white men, the police who are held in contempt by communities of color which have survived much abuse at the hands of police. Do we have a responsibility to theorize the agency or innocence or collusion of these groups, too? When white men make disparaging comments about women of color, do we need to re-present women of color, denounce and replace these representations? If not, are we not merely contributing to the archival representations of disdain that the social science literature has already so horrifically chronicled?

Since all of these participants deserve to be placed within historical and social contexts, and yet power differences and abuses proliferate, how do theorists respect the integrity of informants' consciousness and narratives, place them within social and historical context, and yet not collude in the social scientific gaze, fixation, moral spectacularizing (see Scott, 1997; Roman, 1997) of the poor and working classes? There are no easy answers to these dilemmas. In *The Unknown City* we have tried to contextualize the narratives as spoken within economic, social, and racial contexts so that no one narrator is left holding the bag for his/her demographic group; but indeed there are moments when, within the narratives, "others"—people of color, caseworkers, men, women, the neighbor next door—are portrayed in very disparaging ways. Then we are waged in the battle of *representation*. We work hard to figure out how to represent and contextualize our narrators, ourselves, and the people about whom they are ranting. We try, with the tutelage of historians Joan Scott (1992), Michael Katz (1995), Robin Kelly (1997), and Daryl Scott (1997), sociologist Joyce Ladner (1971), literary critic Eve Sedgwick (1990), and psychologist William Cross (1991), to understand how and why these binaries, these categories of analysis, these "others," these splittings, and these accusations are being cast at this moment in history, and who is being protected by this social science focus on blame (Opotow, 1990). Nevertheless, at times audiences have been alarmed at the language in our texts, at the vivid descriptions and the portraits, for instance, of seemingly cold and heartless social workers. We are working on these issues, and welcome help from others who are also struggling with both theory and empirical data.

What's Safe to Say Aloud . . . and by Whom?

How hard it is for us to *think* we can choose to become writers, much less *feel* and *believe* that we can. What have we to contribute, to give? Our own expectations condition us. Does not our class, our culture as well as the white man tell us writing is not for women such as us?

The white man speaks: *Perhaps if you scrape the dark off your face. Maybe if you bleach your bones. Stop speaking in tongues, stop writing left-handed. Don't cultivate your colored skins nor tongues of fire if you want to make it in a right-handed world.* (Anzaldua, 1981, p. 166)

We have collected stories for the past six years on communities, economic and racial relationships, and individual lives, deeply affected by public policies and institutions that had been rotten and rotting for many years before that. And yet these very same public policies and institutions, the ones about which we have deeply incriminating data, are today being excised; yanked away from communities as we speak. Public schools, welfare, social services, public housing. . . . Positioning a critique of the public sphere as it evaporates, or more aptly, as it is targeted for downsizing and demise, seems an academic waste of time. At its worst, it anticipates collusion with the Right. Nevertheless, the criticisms are stinging.

Tamara: I didn't want to be with the father of my children anymore. And at that time he really gave me a lot of headaches. "If you don't stay with me, then I'm not gonna help you with the kids." Which he really didn't do, which I'm thankful. But I just figured, "Well, the hell with it. Then I'll work . . . get the welfare." Because I pay $640 for this apartment. That's a lot of money for a two bedroom apartment, you know? And the welfare only gives me $424, so I have to make up the difference. And plus I have a telephone, you know. I have cable for my daughters, you know. And it's just a lot of money. And I figure, you know, I figured, well, I couldn't make it on my own. I wasn't making enough to make it on my own back then, so I had to go on welfare. So I did it, and it was . . . I didn't like it. I didn't like sitting there. I didn't like the waiting. I didn't like the questions they asked me, you know?

Mun: What kind of questions did . . .

Tamara: Well, they asked me if I was sexually active, how many times I went to bed with him, you know? And I told the guy, "I'm sorry, but that is none of your business" and I refuse to answer the questions. Because to me, well what, they ask you if you, he asked me if I slept with black men or white men, Puerto Rican men. What was my preference. And to me that was the questions . . .

Mun: Was this on a form, or he . . .

Tamara: No, he was just asking questions, you know? And I refused to answer them, you know. And he kind of like got upset. "We have to ask you this." I was like, "Bullshit." You know, they just wanted to, they asked, he asked me how many times I had sex in a day, and just really, you know, if I douched, if I was clean, if I took a shower. I don't think these are any of your business, you know? I take a shower every night and every day, you know? I think those are stupid questions he asked. I was, he asked me how many men I had in my life that I had, you know, if I have more than one man. And I turned around and told him, "I'm not your mother." I never heard of questions like . . . [laughs]

Mun: Neither have I. [laughs]

Tamara: They asked the weird[est] questions.

Mun: So, how, what was the procedure like?

Tamara: It was embarrassing. Like, with Medicaid, for kids it's good. For kids, you know, you can go anywhere you want with the Medicaid. You can go to the doctors for kids. You know, they pay for braces. When it comes to an adult, I was going to, I was hemorrhaging. I was going to a doctor. I'd been bleeding since December, okay, and they're telling me, I've been going to a gynecologist through the welfare. "It's normal, it's normal. Don't worry about it. It's normal." So last week I was getting ready, for the past week I was feeling really dizzy and really weak, and I said the hell with it. Let me go see a gynecologist. And I paid her. Thank God, you know, the Medicaid took care of the hospital. But I had to pay her $700 for the procedure that I had to have done. [laughs] I had to do it. It was either that or bleed to death, you know. [laughs] But a lot of doctors, I asked her, because she used to take Medicaid. And I asked her, "Why don't you, you know, take Medicaid anymore?" And a lot of doctors that don't, doctors tell you because they don't pay them. She said she's been waiting for people that were on Medicaid to get paid for two years, three years, bills, that's how old the bills are and she's still waiting to get paid.

Our responsibility in this work, as we see it, is not to feed the dismantling of the state by posing a critique of the public sector as it has been, but instead to *insist* on a state that serves well and responsibly its citizenry. That is, social researchers must create vision and imagination for "what could be" and demand the resurrection of an accountable public sphere that has a full and participatory citizenship at its heart. Then we can layer on the critiques of "what has been." That said, it is important to note that it is not so easy when many are just waiting to use our narrative words to do away with welfare; when Brett Schundler, Mayor of Jersey City, is desirous of getting voucher legislation passed in a city in which public schools enjoy little to no positive reputation; when George Gilder and Charles Murray will abduct our phrases as they paint poor women as lazy and irresponsible. Creating a "safe space" for intellectual, critical, and complicated discussion when the Right has been so able and willing to extract arguments that sustain the assault may be a naive, but worthwhile, wish.

ON "SAFE SPACES"

In *The Unknown City* we heard from young women and men who grew up within the working-class and poor segments of our society—how they view economic opportunities, how they spin images of personal and collective futures, especially as related to the power of schooling, how they conceptualize the shrinking public sector, economy, labor, and the military, and how they reflect upon progressive social movements that have historically and dramatically affected their ancestors' and their own life chances. We heard about a disappearing public sphere, but we tripped upon, as well, those urban pockets of counter hegemonic possibility, sites of critique, engagement, and outrage, excavated by these young men and women. Amidst their despair lies hope. And hope appears to be cultivated in these "safe spaces." So how do we write on and through these spaces without romanticizing the tiny corners of sanctuary and possibility available to or created by the poor and working classes in the 1990s? If people are surviving with hope and optimism, is devastation justified or managed?

The spaces into which we have been invited provide recuperation, resistance, and the makings of "home." They are not just a set of geographical-spatial arrangements, but theoretical, analytical, and spatial displacements—a crack, a fissure in an organization or a community. Individual dreams, collective work, and critical thoughts are smuggled in and then reimagined. Not rigidly bounded by walls or fences, the spaces often are corralled by a series of (imaginary) borders where community intrusion and state surveillance are not permitted. These are spaces where trite social stereotypes are fiercely contested. That is, these young women and men, in their constant confrontation with harsh public representations of *their* race, ethnic, class, gender, and sexuality, use these spaces to break down these public images for scrutiny and to invent new ones.

These spaces include the corners of the African American church where young men ponder how to "take back the streets" to "save the young boys"; the lesbian and gay center carved out quietly by working-class late adolescents and young adults, seeking identities and networks when their geographic and cultural contexts deny them sexual expression; the Head Start and EPIC (Every Person Influences Children) programs in which poor mothers, and sometimes fathers, come together to talk about the delights and the minefields of raising children in a culture showered in racism and decimated by poverty; the cultural arts programs where men and women join self-consciously across racial and ethnic borders to create what is "not yet," a space, a set of images, a series of aesthetic products that speak of a world that could be (Weis & Fine, 2000).

Spaces such as these spring from the passions and concerns of community members; they are rarely structured from "above." They may be a onetime fiction, transitory or quite stable. They can be designed to restore identities devastated by the larger culture or they may be opportunities to try on identities and community rejected by both mainstream culture and local ethnic groups. These spaces hold rich and revealing data about the resilience of young adults, without denying the oppression which threatens the borders and interiors of community life amidst urban poverty.

Legitimately one may ask (and some have) whether we have any business floating through or writing about these sequestered quarters. Does our presence affect or interrupt the music of life within "free spaces"? Does our social scientific voyeurism shatter the sanctity of that which is presumably (although recognizably *not*) "free"?

We come down on these questions, for the moment at least, by presenting two different incidents. One occurred in a basement office in which New Jersey community activists met to discuss local politics. We were welcomed for the initial interview, but the notion of our continued presence clearly provoked a discomfort. Not asked to return, we left—in good stead and with enormous respect. In contrast, for instance, we have been invited into some spaces (e.g., EPIC parenting group, black church, community center, lesbian and gay club) in which members, directors, and others indicate they are eager for documentation—anxious for others to know who they "really" are, what functions the programs serve, how deeply spiritual and religious "those teenage mothers" can be, how organized and supportive "those gays and lesbians" are. They have welcomed us into their spaces to "exploit" our capacity—our class and professional positions and networks—and our willingness to write and to testify to those aspects of community life that the media ignore, that stereotypes deny, that mainstream culture rarely gets to see. And yet we seek not to romanticize resilience—for these spaces represent severe critique as well as warm comfort.

ON RESPONSIBILITIES

We have certainly read much, and even written a fair amount, about researchers' subjectivities (Fine, 1994). Our obligation is to come clean "at the hyphen," meaning that we interrogate in our writings who *we* are as we coproduce the narratives we presume to collect, and we anticipate how the public and policy makers will receive, distort, misread our data. It is now acknowledged that we critical ethnographers have a responsibility to talk about our identities, why we interrogate what we do, what we choose not to report, how we frame our data, on whom we shed our scholarly gaze, who is protected and not protected as we do our work. What is our participatory responsibility to research with and for a more progressive community life? As part of this discussion, we want to try to explain how we, as researchers, have worked with communities to capture and build upon exciting community and social movements. In other words, we will put forward parts of our ever evolving political agenda, sharing the kinds of scholarship and action that we are focusing upon and how our work has been reshaped by the activism in the communities studied.

Thus far, in Jersey City and Buffalo, we have been able to document how state policies and local economic/social shifts have affected young women and men's belief systems, world views, social consciousness. Through individual interviews we have gathered much of this information. Through the focus groups, for example, in the Lesbian and Gay Club, in the African American and white churches, in the EPIC parenting group, in the Latino homeless shelter, in the Pre-Cap college program for young adolescents, we have been able to create settings in which our interviewees have begun to weave together analyses about their commitments, for instance, to the "next generation of African American boys," or to "practicing the ways of my grandmother" around Latino spiritual rituals. An activist nun and a local director of Head Start have both invited us to work more closely with groups of women and men in their programs, running focus groups that would raise questions, press issues, and help the participants reshape programs. A college preparation program for "at risk" youths (labels!) asked us for an evaluation to assist with further funding. In the EPIC group, we were told that the engagement of several members was raised due to the kind of individual and group work we were involved in. For these women, the group interviews offered a way of piecing together the strengths of their lives, encouraging forward movement as they were raising their families in the midst of poverty. Indeed, Lois Weis was asked to facilitate an EPIC group on a long-term basis.

Further, throughout the course of our five years of research, we have moved across the researcher-researched hyphen, and into a community of activists, to apply our work to support local policy and community efforts. Michelle testified at state hearings in Trenton and in Jersey City on the "State Takeover of the Local Schools," advocating with community groups that the state remain in control until authentic local participation can be encouraged and sustained; Mun Wong coordinated a project among women on welfare who were eager to document the differential supermarket prices of similar items, at different points in the month and in different markets in the community; Lois Weis supplied testimony in support of continual funding for EPIC; and in Jersey City, we have provided census and qualitative data to city council members from the Latino community. Our graduate students have been deeply involved in various communities as they engage in dissertation work in an Irish community center, an African American church, a neighborhood center which serves white working-class youth, a neighborhood arts center, and numerous other community groups. In all such spaces, graduate students are giving back to the communities in which they are working. Across communities, numerous conversations have taken place with key policy makers on a number of issues arising from our data.

We take for granted that the purpose of social inquiry at the turn of the century is not only to generate new knowledge but to reform "common sense" and critically inform public policies, existent social movements, and daily community life. A commitment to such "application," however, should not be taken for granted. This is a critical moment in the life of the social sciences, one in which individual scholars are today making decisions about the extent to which our work should aim to be "useful."

We have colleagues who embrace the commitment to application, as we do, even if some think it is naive to imagine being able to infiltrate current policy talk on life within poor and working-class communities; other colleagues have long seen their own scholarship as explicitly aimed toward political and social change (see the work of Gittell, 1990, 1994; Piven &

Cloward, 1971; Lykes, 1994; Mullings, 1984; Powell, 1994). And yet we hear a growing chorus of colleagues (on the Right and Left) who presume that if you are interested in, engaged by, or drawn to policy, your scholarship is less trustworthy, tainted by advocacy, commitments, passion, or responsibilities. This latter position was perhaps in retreat for a moment in time, but it seems to be returning to the academy in well-orchestrated volume. We do, of course, reject this latter position, but would ask again that academics who see their work as deeply nested in community life (recognizing the notion of "community" is up for grabs) come together to argue cogently their responses to the litany: "Is this science? Is this advocacy? Is only progressive work biased? Is this politics or policy?"

We must probe to find the sites of intellectual leverage, responsibility, and obligation through which our work can begin to fissure public and political discourse, shifting the ideological and material grounds on which poor and working-class men and women are now being tortured. That said, we take our responsibilities to these communities seriously, and Lois Weis and Michelle Fine are educating their graduate students to work with, not on or despite, local community efforts.

It is important to note another underground debate within community studies which concerns the tension between representing historically oppressed groups as "victimized" and "damaged" *or* as "resilient" and "strong." This may seem an artificial and dangerous dichotomy—we think it is. But we have encountered colleagues within feminism, "critical race theory," poverty work, disability studies, and most recently queer theory, arguing across these intellectual stances, with these two choices carved out as the (presumably only) appropriate alternatives. We share the worries, but worry more about the fixed choices that are being offered. Simple stories of victimization, with no evidence of resistance, resilience, or agency are seriously flawed and deceptively partial, and they deny the rich subjectivities of persons surviving amidst devastating social circumstances. Equally dreary, however, are the increasingly popular stories of individual heroes who thrive in spite of and denying the burdens of surviving amidst such circumstances.

We stretch toward writing that spirals around social injustice and resilience; that recognizes the endurance of structures of injustice and the powerful acts of agency; that appreciates the courage and the limits of individual acts of resistance, but refuses to perpetuate the fantasy that "victims" are simply powerless. That these women and men are strong *is not evidence that they have suffered no oppression.* Individual and collective strength cannot be used against poor and working-class people as evidence of "See—it's not been so bad!" We need to invent an intellectual stance in which structural oppression, passion, social movements, evidence of strength, health, and "damage" can all be recognized and theorized without erasing essential features of the complex story of injustice that constitutes urban life in poverty.

We take solace in the words of many of our African American male informants—drawn from churches and spiritual communities—who testify, "Only belief and hope will save our communities. We have come a long, long way . . . and we have much further to go. Only belief will get us through." Amidst the pain, the despair, survives hope. This, too, is a big part of community life, rarely seen in the light of day.

We end this essay with a set of what might be called ethical invitations or, put more boldly, ethical injunctions. We offer these in the spirit of wedging open and contributing to a conversation about researcher responsibility, recognizing, of course, that questions of responsibility-for-whom will, and should, forever be paramount: because the "whom" is not a coherent whole—no single constituency, unified community, group, or set of "others"—and because the context in which we write today will change tomorrow, and so, too, will the readings of this text.

We write on the ethics of responsibility because we don't want to write only for and with friends; we hope to write in ways that contribute to a reshaping of the "common sense" about poverty, the economy, and social and human relations. We consider, then, the ethics of writing research in the interest of social justice and the ethics of publishing what Richardson (1995) has called "writing-stories." We offer the ideas below as lenses through which social analyses might be continually assessed and (re)imagined.

On Reframing What Seems Like Good and Bad News

Our first injunction holds that social researchers dare to speak hard truths with a theoretical rigor and political savvy. By that, we mean that "bad stories," like "good stories," are always partial but/and deserve a hearing. They reveal as much as they conceal—whether informants seem too close or too far. Having witnessed the Right-wing assault on education, health care, welfare, and immigration in this country, we have become more convinced, not less, that progressive activists and researchers need to interrogate with deliberation—not camouflage with romance—some of the rough spots in our work. To obscure the bad news is to fool no one. Indeed, the suffocation of bad stories only tempers the very real stories of oppression we seek to tell. That there are (unevenly distributed) damaging consequences to all living under advanced capitalism, racist social relations, violent gendered relations, and homophobic community life is no great secret. That individuals engage in activities or behaviors deemed illegal, unethical, immoral in contexts in which justice and fairness have no role, is evidence of social injustice—not a reason to blame victims. That many thrive despite the odds is equally well known. How survival, damage, and oppressive social/economic relations meld together is the task of explanation that lies before us. How to inform and encourage social movements for "what could be" is the task at hand. Thus, indeed, we err on the side of telling many kinds of stories, attached always to history, larger structures, and social forces, offered neither to glamorize nor to pathologize, but to *re*-view what has been, to *re*-imagine what could be in communities of poverty and the working class, and to *re*-visit, with critical speculation, lives, relations, and communities of privilege.

Upon Reflections

We ask, second, that beginning and veteran researchers, and all of us in between, pose a set of questions to ourselves as we move through the recursive "stages" of social analysis. These questions are listed in no particular order and have few right answers. But, we insist, they should be asked as we all write what we write in a world not (necessarily) prepared to hear.

  • *Have I connected the "voices" and "stories" of individuals back to the set of historic, structural, and economic relations in which they are situated?* We mean this in no linear fashion, in no simple determinative progression, but simply to recognize that what people say has a relation to the structures and ideologies around them in ways that will almost certainly not be narrated by interviewees themselves. The work of theory is to articulate these relations, excavating how qualitative narratives or even quantitative responses on a 5-point Likert scale are nested within a system of historic and material conditions.

  • *Have I deployed multiple methods so that very different kinds of analyses can be constructed?* As mentioned earlier, in our research for *The Unknown City* (1998), individual and focus-group interviews generated very different kinds of narration—neither more true than the other, but different, particularly when it came to expressing optimism or pessimism about the future and one's place in it. We came to understand that it was important to theorize why and how responses took different forms, seeking not simple confirmation, nor concluding too easily that there is contradiction or that one narration is more "true" than the other. Instead, we struggled to cultivate a theoretical relation between possibly very different responses, understanding that the issue of *triangulation* is not simple. Different people do, in fact, seem the same but different at times. The same person can do likewise. We cannot see this as contradictory or, worse, useless data causing us to miss important facets of individual and community life.

• *Have I described the mundane?* As we have noted, the temptation to surf through our transcripts with a coding eye toward the exotic or the violent is hard to resist. Coding tends to lend itself to that. And yet most of our transcriptions detail the boring details of life on the ground, day-to-day interactions with friends, kin, neighbors, children, and television. These portraits, though rarely stunning, constitute much of life in poverty and should not be relegated to the edited-out files.

• *Have some informants/constituencies/participants reviewed the material with me, interpreted, dissented, challenged my interpretations? And then how do I report these departures/agreements in perspective?* This is not a call for handing over veto power—but only a call for conversation, negotiated interpretations, texts in which multiple interpretations flourish, in which challenges are integrated into the manuscript. Much of this work can take place in follow-up focus groups to either participant observation work or individual interviews.

• *How far do I want to go with respect to theorizing the words of informants?* That is, with respect to what Fine and Weis (1996) have called the "triple representation problem," have I worked to understand my contribution to the materials/narrations provided and those silenced? Have I worked to explain to readers the position from which informants speak? Have I worked to recast the person(s) whom the informant chooses to blame or credit for social justice (be it a social worker, one's mother, black men)? Again, we do not hold out that all researchers must answer yes to these questions—only that we researchers (faculty and graduate students) must ask ourselves these questions and understand *why* it is that some answers must be "no."

• *Have I considered how these data could be used for progressive, conservative, repressive social policies?* How might the data be heard? Misread? Misappropriated? Do I need to add a "warning" about potential misuse?

- *Where have I backed into the passive voice and decoupled my responsibility for my interpretations?* That is, where have I hidden my own "author-ity" behind *their* narrations or *their* participatory interpretations?
- *Who am I afraid will see these analyses?* Who is rendered vulnerable, responsible or exposed by these analyses? Am I willing to show him/her/them the text before publication? If not, why not? Could I publish his/her/their comments as an epilogue? What is the fear?
- *What dreams am I having about the material presented?* What issues are pulling at, or out of, my own biography? Have I over- or underplayed them?
- *To what extent has this analysis offered an alternative to the "common sense" or dominant discourse?* What challenges might very different audiences pose to the analysis presented?

None of the above questions is intended to stifle scholarly license nor to insist that there is one right way to answer them, but instead to expand our work by recognizing the potential influence of our writings: the pulls, fantasies, projections, and likely responses of very different kinds of audiences and, therefore, the responsibility we have to anticipate the relation between the texts we produce and the "common sense" that awaits or confronts them. By asking ourselves the above questions, we push the issues, forcing ourselves to deal with what are serious dilemmas in our research. We repeat, not all of us will answer the same way. But we will clarify why we answer the way we do.

On Cautions

After reflections, we suggest that particularly those of us who write on questions of structural relations to the micropolitics of life in poverty, draft and publish a "Legend of Cautions: Ways to Misread, Misappropriate, and Misuse Presented Analyses." That is, we imagine such a legend which warns readers of how not to read our work, for example, how not to use evidence of welfare fraud to cut payments or resurrect a welfare surveillance system, how not to exploit the real fears inside poor communities to generate support for the building of more prisons, how not to appropriate the anger of poor communities at their public schools as a rallying cry for vouchers likely to serve few but the relatively privileged. We recommend many, many drafts of these "Warnings" . . . but anticipate that without these warnings the likelihood of our analyses being misappropriated is much higher than the likelihood of our analyses being deployed for ends that we would approve.

On Educating Our Students in Multiple Genres

We exit this essay with our most fierce injunction—that we have an ethical responsibility to retreat from the stance of dispassion all too prevalent in the academy and to educate our students toward analyzing, writing, and publishing in multiple genres at one and the same time: in policy talk, in the voices of empiricism, through the murky swamps of self-reflective "writing-stories," and in the more accessible languages of pamphlets, fliers, and community booklets. That is, if we are serious about enabling our students to be fluent across methods, engaged with community struggles, and theorizing conditions of social (in)justice, we must recognize that flickers and movements for social change happen in varied sites—courtrooms, legislative offices, the media, community-based organizations, and church groups, as well as the academy—and therefore through varied texts.

We full well recognize that there may be consequences for nontenured faculty who attempt to write across audience in the way we are suggesting. Tenure review committees and external reviewers associated with these committees may not "count" writing other than traditional research (including qualitative analyses) as evidence of an individual deserving of tenure or later promotion to full professor. It is important for junior faculty to establish credibility within a traditional research community. As one writes for a scholarly audience, however, it is possible to exercise simultaneously the option for writing in multiple tongues. We are not urging graduate students and junior faculty to write for broad-based audiences at the expense of writing for scholarly journals, authoring monographs, and so forth. While the academy is changing, we recognize the moves are slow, and resistance is always high.

With this caveat in mind, reflections on our responsibilities as social researchers must punctuate all texts we produce. Without such reflection, in the name of neutrality or researcher dispassion, we collude in a retreat from social responsibility and the academy remains yet another institution without a soul in a world increasingly bankrupt of moral authority.

CHAPTER 4

REFLECTIONS ON THE POLITICS AND METHODS OF QUALITATIVE WORK

In this chapter we offer, to students new to qualitative work and to those of us who have been engaged in such practice for many years, a cacophony of troubles and thoughts related to ongoing work in what we call "safe spaces" in urban America. As a cross-campus (SUNY and CUNY) collective, most of the graduate students who write here have been supported in one form or another by our grants from the Spencer and Carnegie foundations to conduct qualitative research with youth and young adults in urban communities, focused at the intersections of life histories, social relations, and political movements. Some are engaged in interview projects with individuals, focus groups, and/or participant observation studies. Many of those who write have completed or are now completing their dissertations. Most are conducting research in sites which Boyte and Evans have called "free spaces," spaces for identity work or political change, spaces of course never fully free, but carved for imagination nonetheless (Weis & Fine, 2000). These spaces may be geographic, as in squatters taking back public housing or urban youth taking back their schools; they may be spiritual, as in religious diasporas or churches; they may be social-movement based, as in the lesbian, gay, and bisexual movements or the civil rights movements; they may be for the body or aesthetic, as in sports, community arts, or martial arts. Finally, these spaces may simply be yearned for, sought, and rarely found, as in the constant search for safe spots for honest talk about sexuality, mothering, race relations, and immigration.

In doing work that cuts across a range of methods, units of analysis, and sites, toward a common theoretical frame (Weis & Fine, 2000), we enter with distinct subjectivities, bump into varied obstacles to the study, and seek to co-construct very different kinds of empirical materials. But we all hit speed bumps. Our bumps range from finding our political investments and identities nestled too intimately inside the narratives of men and women whom we have interviewed, to the troubles of gaining ethics approval from academic committees seemingly more concerned with institutional liability than the work at hand, to the struggle of (co)constructing narratives that challenge—rather than reproduce—dominant discourses, to the profound delicacies of conducting commissioned, critical research within self-inquiring institutions like urban schools or an AIDS services organization where gatekeepers decide, perhaps, that they do not want to hear what they paid us to see. And so we offer these stories, told by graduate students, with an invitation for reflection on how and why we do work on social injustice and social possibility, when to speak and remain silent, and how to code, analyze, and write.

This chapter represents collective effort as students met and drafted at SUNY and CUNY, read and reread essays at their respective campuses, and we read across campus, offered feedback to each writer, and ultimately pulled the essay together. In each "space," issues raised in Chapter 3 of this volume were discussed extensively as they relate to each of the individual studies.

LOOKING IN THE MIRROR:
DANGER—OBJECTS MAY BE CLOSER
THAN THEY APPEAR

A number of us are engaged in research conducted with and for respondents who share our political investments and identities, our standpoints, and our cultural biographies. As we toil inside these quite familiar fields, we are at once attracted to and worried about studying persons whose lives, passions, and politics coalesce so neatly with our own.

We write in this section about insider/outsider dilemmas, with some fears that, like those "objects" in our rear view mirror, the subjects of study may be "closer" or "further" than they appear. We use each other, and members of our research worlds, as interpretive communities, advisors, or guides, to assure that our critical eyes do not wander astray at significant if discomforting junctures in our work. In this section, both Kenneth Foster and Susan Lombardo narrate how he and she have wandered through the familiar, so enjoying the intimacies of political solidarity with civil rights activists and with Irish Americans, and yet deliberately stretching to see the distinctions within. Kathleen C. Tocke, in contrast, assumed she had little in common with inner city teenage women and learned instead about "equal access" to sexual harassment. Craig Centrie, too, learned he can share more across class lines than he realized. Tracy A. McFarlane learned that she is not quite the insider to Jamaican consciousness that she had assumed she was when she began her research.

YOU'RE BREAKING MY HEART, BUT I MUST EDIT YOUR LIFE: MY WORK, MY ROAD, MY BUMPS

Kenneth Foster

Speed bumps are usually strategically and systematically placed on the road. They are impediments to travel at rates of speed that may at the moment be ill advised. Sometimes their intent is to slow you down because the area you have entered needs to be moved through cautiously. Other times, speed bumps are warning signals, alerting us that we have veered off the road—we have not seen what we were supposed to see.

In the midst of a qualitative investigation of racism and empowerment, as perceived by African American civil rights and social activists, my goals included gaining an understanding of how such individuals view racism in their biographies and how racism provoked their activism (see Figure 4.1).

I'm an academic and a social scientist—ostensibly on equal footing with my white peers. But in the work I am profoundly aware that I do not experience disparities of material goods, origins, social location, or power with my participants, whom Alcoff can call "others" (Alcoff & Gray, 1993). I find I cannot consider "them" to be "others."

Like my informants, I am black, I am a witness to and a victim of racism, I have engaged in numerous civil rights movements and consider

FIGURE 4.1. Summary of Research Project

The relationship between racism and psychological or personal empowerment among African Americans, particularly as manifest in civil rights activism, remains unclear. This qualitative research project will collect data on and describe some of the conditions under which African Americans become empowered. A sample of 20 African American activists are being interviewed in various locations in New York, New Jersey, and Pennsylvania.

A semistructured questionnaire is being used to collect data on experiences with and perceptions of racism and empowerment. It is anticipated that such individuals perceive racism as a pervasive threat to their psychological well-being and that their activist attitudes and behaviors are, at least in part, a response to this threat.

---

myself an activist. My research participants are people of my generation, my race, my ethnicity, my education level. They have roots and relatives in the southeast United States whose names and recipes, stories and re- unions are the same as mine. In essence, I am both "us" and "them." The bumps that I feel are, in part, from the familiarity, the identification, the sameness of thought. A major challenge for me is to dismember—that is, code and edit—the complex web of voices, reverberances, and echoes that comprise their lives and mine. I find myself resisting the coding and edit- ing. Because it hits so close to home, it feels as if a slice of my life falls on the cutting room floor along with my participants.

So at the bump I am struck by how much I talk in these interviews. With embarrassment, I listen to my tapes (of interviews), and it seems I have shared nearly as much with my participants as they have with me. "I know what you mean. Just the other day, I . . . ." Clearly interrupting a flow of thoughts, ideas, and recollections on the part of participants, I could also be unwittingly introducing a threat to the validity—or what Patti Lather (1991) refers to as the "trustworthiness"—of my material. In my zeal to connect, participants become active and critical listeners to my stories, perhaps editing and shaping their subsequent remarks based on my ran- dom recollections. The challenge is to grip the wheel, not too tightly or loosely, periodically check the rearview mirror, see (and hear) what lies before me, and keep my eyes on the road.

ON FRECKLES AND ACCESS

Susan Lombardo

I am Irish, with an appearance that is perhaps stereotypical: red hair, freckles, and sensitivity to the sun. My one previous attempt at exploring my Irishness left me with some discomfort when I went to Ireland several years ago in search of my "roots." While I, admittedly, found the country to be beautiful, my connection seemed to end there. I guess I had expected some sort of metamorphosis during my visit, and the truth of the matter is that I felt nothing.

But when I began to study Irish people for my dissertation, the more I "hung around" them, the more Irish I seemed to become. In fact, my com- mittee chairperson remarked that I was looking more and more Irish (if that's possible) as my project progressed. During data collection, I identi- fied with these people, many times even wearing the Irish sweaters and *claddagh* rings (the hallmark of "Irishness," which symbolize friendship, loyalty, and love) I had tucked away after my trip to Ireland. I reasoned that these things allowed me to move about freely in the Irish Center, the site for my study, and, indeed, they did work to my advantage. But what was really happening was a process of identification.

In retrospect, I shouldn't have been surprised by my behavior because identification has crossed my path before. I recall, for example, that when I was a nursing student doing my psychiatric rotation, I became convinced that I was schizophrenic. Or, when working with cancer patients, that I had cancer. Once I got away from the psychiatric or the cancer patients, I'd be my old self.

But I can't escape my Irishness. I assimilated into the culture in a way I had not believed possible. I dined with them, danced with them, volunteered with them, cried with them during the dedication of the famine memorial monument, and even saw my beloved deceased father in the eyes of the old Irish men who frequented the Irish Center.

The participants became my allies, I, their confidant. They were my social club. All of my leisure time was spent with them, and the need to protect them was ever growing. They welcomed and enveloped me with such fervor that I was seduced with an intensity I cannot describe. I was, for the first time in my life, with people who looked a lot like me. My red hair and freckles were now an asset, not a mark of difference.

In my study group at the university, someone pointed out things about the Irish that I knew, in part, to be descriptive but less than complimentary. At every turn I defended them, becoming the protector. It had become (shockingly) clear that to insult them and to point out their inadequacies was to insult me and my inadequacies.

While I had been "caught up" in the whole process, I now realize that my heart and my soul does not feel as strongly connected to "Irishness" as do the participants. I don't feel an allegiance to Ireland, its causes, or its tragedies. I don't like Irish food, and most of the music does not move me at all. But I also discovered that I am no longer empty in a cultural sense. I enjoy a new respect for Irish people, my ancestry, and traditions. Much of the Irish poetry, dance, and literary works do, in fact, move me, and perhaps I have walked away from the experience knowing myself a little better.

Is it possible that, because I had been so caught up in being Irish, I missed certain critical points necessary to my dissertation which hinge upon whiteness? Probably. But these omissions are not irreversible. I know where the critical points are and have relocated them. My seduction was, after all, latent and temporary.

SEXUALLY HARASSING BUMPS

Kathleen C. Tocke

Karyna, a student at Turner Vocational School, and I walked through the quiet hallway. The bell rang and seconds later I was introduced, or rather thrown into, the world of a young woman attending a predominantly male, inner-city high school. My ears perked up in utter amazement as teenage boys made extraordinarily sexist comments and primitive noises as we passed through the hall. After a few moments, I was struck with the realization that they were directed, not just at Karyna, but at me as well. My education at an all-girls high school had not prepared me for this. There I was, a young graduate student new to the field, trying to be professional, yet I was accorded the same lack of respect as the 15- and 16-year-olds I was interviewing. The days that followed brought even more remarks and sexist gestures. I saw girls tickled, poked, and groped. Like the young women students, I found myself not immune to the unwelcome attention, but ignoring it so as not to attract any more attention.

How to dress for a day at Turner became one of my bigger concerns. Before I began the study, I had debated what to wear to the interviews, how I could "fit in" a little more. After just one day at the site, I learned what *not* to wear: anything that indicated that I might have some semblance of a female body. While I lacked the rounded and well-endowed figure preferred by many of the young men in the school, the mere fact that I lacked male genitalia entitled me to sexual harassment.

For the first time, I found myself unable to respond to comments regarding the legs that are attached to my thin 5'9" frame. I was unable to respond to the "oh, baby's" and the stares that made me feel like a rump roast in a meat market. I was disappointed in myself, but what could I say? Here I was walking with these young women, I wanted to set an example, but what example would that be? Could I have acted the part of the strong woman by questioning or reprimanding their comments and gestures? That would only have attracted more attention and delighted and aroused the boys more. What would the young women have thought if I had said something? What right did I have as an outsider in their school to assert myself? Would I be belittling these young women who felt they couldn't oppose the harassment that they faced day after day? At the same time, I wondered what they thought of me because I didn't defend myself.

Looking back on my time at Turner, I realize that I was asking the same questions as the young women I had interviewed. The words of one student still linger in my mind. Tonya, a 17-year-old senior and single mother, was explaining "just how tough" it is for young women at Turner. She was speaking of a time when a male student approached her and remarked that the only reason her baby's father had stayed with her for three years was because she must have "good stuff." Revolted by the crudeness of the remark, Tonya told me she had said to herself, "I don't know whether to slap you or go on about my business and just know that you are ignorant, saying what you're saying."

It was difficult for me, a woman in my early twenties, to deal with the situation, but I understand more how much harder it must be for an adolescent to cope with the situation day after day with people who are her peers. Perhaps I was naive to think that I would have nothing in common with these young inner-city girls. I never imagined that I would connect with them in this way, yet I was facing the same dilemma that many of them faced every day in their school. Like them, I could offer no solution, make no effective reprimands, or completely justify my silence. I felt hopelessly unable to change anything.

Although sexual harassment may have become normalized in this school and the young women accustomed to the ways of the boys in the classrooms and hallways, they are still looking for their own answers in the hectic world of the American teenager. I find myself frustrated, searching for my own answer, knowing that sexual harassment does not end after adolescence.

(RE-)LOCATING PARADISE

Craig Centrie

When I was little, people said I was nosey. It's really no surprise that I became an ethnographer as an adult. My nosiness has taken me to many places and, on occasion during a site visit, I have been frightened, wondering how I was going to get out of a predicament unscathed.

Over the last 6 years, I have been involved in a large research project called "Reconciling the Voices of Hope and Despair" funded by the Spencer Foundation. Through long in-depth interviews in Buffalo, New York, and Jersey City, over 150 young adults, most poor or working-class, narrated their life experiences in the post-Reagan period and a withering public sphere. Many of my narrators would be my neighbors or people I've seen hanging out.

In the middle of the summer, the second-floor interviewing room was sweltering. I thought I would melt. I wanted the interview to start promptly.

Fifteen minutes later, as I was about to pack up my stuff and go, cheerful and plump Carlos appeared at the head of the stairs. I had an attitude.

Carlos was handsome in a boyish sort of way, giving him an air of mischievousness. He waddled a little when he walked, which only added to his jovial appearance. His personality was disarming and infectious. After the usual introductions and pleasantries, I had changed moods and returned to my curious self, wondering what made Carlos so contented.

The interview began as all of them did, with questions about background family life and growing up. Carlos grew up in a small village in Puerto Rico. He began by telling of the small house and farm on which he grew up. There were elegant and descriptive passages which focused on beautiful scenery, royal palm trees, fields of undulating sugar cane, and a luxuriant, meandering stream that he crossed every day on his way to school. I noticed, though, despite the creative description of idyllic scenes, Carlos displayed none of the mythical nostalgia many "Nuyoricans" speak of when reminiscing on Puerto Rico. In many of the other interviews, Puerto Rican immigrants, when reflecting on a Puerto Rico of their childhood, remember and long for a loving and familiar motherland, a place both beautiful and secure. Most of all, it was a place of belonging. Carlos spoke of abject poverty and cruel physical and verbal abuse. There was the suggestion of sexual abuse by an older male cousin. Most of all, he remembered never being loved by anyone. No matter how hard he tried to please his aunt, he could remember nothing but severe ridicule, impossible demands for money, and the worst farm work. He spoke of miserable nights awake on a cot, both hungry and lonely, crying himself to sleep. The sparkling and meandering stream he spoke of earlier became a difficult barrier to cross with no shoes. The days at school, when he could attend, were filled with memories of hunger while watching other children eat food prepared lovingly by mothers who awaited them at home.

During accounts of both abuse and nights of crying, Carlos became flush and began to quietly sob. After each episode, he would politely apologize and continue with his narration. He said that, at some point in his teenage years, he was able to accumulate enough money to pay for a trip to the States where he would stay with a sister. Things for him appeared to improve. He found work and a better life. After several years, he returned to Puerto Rico to a little town and farm he remembered. He wanted to make a positive impression on his aunt. Perhaps he could make sense of what happened to him and bring it all to a good end. On his arrival, he was greeted with distance and disdain. Yet he persisted. In the end, all his money was stolen from him and he was sent away.

At this point in his narration, Carlos began to cry uncontrollably. I felt dumbstruck. It is not my nature to be emotional. I felt as if I wanted to cry as well, but did not. Further, this was a new experience in an interview, and I had no idea what I was expected to do. Other than to say a few comforting words, I didn't do anything. At the end of his narration, Carlos asked if he could see me again, could he make another appointment. He remarked that he found the session to be very therapeutic and that he felt it did him a world of good. No one, he remarked, had ever listened to him in this way before. I explained that I wasn't a therapist. In fact, I knew nothing about it. But this question concerned me.

We left the building together. I noticed that he was out of breath as he walked. I asked if he was alright. He mentioned he had a bad case of asthma. He was nervous about the interview, causing it to flare up earlier in the day. That was why he was late. The emotional narrations of his past caused him to feel asthmatic again. In the long run, though, Carlos confided that he felt he had finally confronted some issues today and that he would begin to deal with them.

As we walked out of the building, I knew this was it. I would have to say good-bye. It seemed like a heartless ending. I felt guilty about getting into my car and leaving him. Seeing him struggle with his breathing, I quickly made a decision to offer him a ride home. He was thankful, making sure it wasn't an inconvenience. He lived only a few minutes away deeper into Buffalo's West Side, across Niagara Street. He took me through a maze of narrow one-way streets filled with small cottages, many built around the time of the Civil War, most in varying degrees of ruin. There was a great deal of debris around, garbage really. In the park were about ten young Latino males talking in rapid succession. Several men and a woman were strolling down the street, sharing a bottle in a brown paper bag and speaking in a staccato Spanish. It was stifling hot and there was a smell of stale liquor and urine in the air.

Carlos instructed me to pull over. In the midst of this scene of urban blight, there was a single workman's cottage much like the others we had seen on the way. I parked, and Carlos asked me if I wanted to sit on the porch for a few minutes. I got out. Several hypodermic needles crunched under my feet. We went up the stairs and I took a seat on some kitchen furniture while Carlos went inside to bring out some soda. I noticed that this house was a little different than the others. Although old and in need of some repairs, it was freshly painted and very neat. The kitchen furniture was not just thrown randomly, but arranged. Next to the cottage was a beautiful fenced garden with vegetables of all kinds and flowers—marigolds, zinnias, and alyssum. On the side of the porch was a trellised old red rose. This little house had something special. It had warmth and permanence. It was a home.

Carlos came out and handed me a big glass of homemade lemonade. We sat there for some time. No one said anything. I was marveling at the vegetables, the roses, and the herbs. Finally, I exclaimed how beautiful everything was. He looked delighted that I noticed. I asked him some questions. Politely he responded to each question. He commented that times had gotten bad for him in New York City. He had heard of easier cities to live in upstate and came here. He bought this house for only $5,000. It was home. It gave him a sense of meaning, purpose, and belonging he had searched for all his life. He said he found paradise. Here, away from pressure, he was at ease. Over the last two years, his relationship with his girlfriend improved. He proudly announced they would be getting together again. The three of them (his girlfriend has a baby) would live here. He seemed contented and at peace with himself. Even his asthmatic wheezing disappeared as he talked of his home and his future.

We stopped talking for a moment. I looked over the railing. A tall, disheveled woman was coming down the street. She moved quickly and nervously. She had a blank, almost haunted expression on her face. She was a crack cocaine user desperately searching for her next fix, a flight over the rainbow. She was ugly. Life made her ugly. It was the kind of ugliness that oozed and seeped from one's pores. She walked rapidly down the street wearing her ugliness with conviction. She passed us and yelled "Hey, boys, some good pussy here. Best pussy in town." We silently shook our heads no, looking down from paradise. She never bothered to look up, having anticipated a familiar response.

Carlos and I sat silently a few more minutes. Neither of us had anything more to say. We never acknowledged the crack head, the hype, the ghost. I put my glass down, stood, shook his hand, said thank-you. It was sincere. I meant it. I gained something. This experience with Carlos made all of my worries unimportant and selfish.

I also pondered my role as an ethnographer. How easily and effortlessly I move in and out of diverse communities. I take so much for granted. Most of all as an ethnographer, I walk in and out of people's lives. I spend an hour with them listening; they spill their guts, telling their life story. Sometimes I feel as if I have nothing to offer to them in return. Perhaps, as in the case with Carlos, just listening in a nonjudgmental way is very important. For me, each new interview is a new important facet of life. It's something that helps me understand the world I live in and my place in it. Through Carlos, I got a better understanding of that paradise.

(DIS)REGARDING RACE

Tracy A. McFarlane

On the day I presented my idea for my master's thesis I was excited at the opportunity to share in class the kernel of an idea I had just begun to develop. I began:

> I'm interested in studying the factors that influence well-being for Jamaican immigrants who live in New York City, with particular focus on those resources that foster resilience. The literature suggests that migration is a major stressor, and most of the early work has highlighted the debilitating effects of moving from one country to live in another. Immigrants of color have been portrayed as being particularly vulnerable, yet I know many immigrants who will tell you that despite the stress of adjusting to life in a new country, they have experienced benefits from having made this transition. I think it is important to do a more balanced assessment of the immigration experience, one that allows for telling both sides of the story.

A stimulating discussion followed, during which my colleagues asked me questions and made suggestions that helped me clarify my research question. I was feeling very fortunate to have the opportunity to develop my ideas among such a supportive, clever group until one critical thinker asked: "What about race?"

"*What* about race?" I countered.

"Well, Jamaicans are immigrants of color. They are going to have certain experiences because of their race, and this may, in turn, have some effect on their well-being. Are you going to include that in your study?"

Around the table people were nodding their heads, murmuring in agreement as they turned to me for my response. I bristled at the inquiry, thinking that perhaps I was not so fortunate to be here, after all. My too-dark-to-show-a-blush cheeks grew warm as I responded:

> Look, when Jamaicans move here, they know they are black, but they're coming from a society in which their race has not been a deterrent to accomplishing their goals. They are accustomed to seeing people who look like them in power and in positions of authority. What they face at home is poverty and discrimination based on their socio-economic status or class, but not their race. They see America as the place where more economic opportunities exist. They are not going to let other people's prejudices prevent their progress!

The frustration I felt at that point had several sources. As a Jamaican immigrant myself, I was resistant to addressing racism directly, since I could not do so without acknowledging tensions between American-born ethnic minorities and immigrants of color. This matter is a personal sore point for me, since I believe history has shown within-race discrimination only serves to impede our progress and advance the interests of those who oppose racial equality. In addition, I was impatient at having to point out, yet again, that people of color are more than their color. Sometimes we don't want to be portrayed as victims, vulnerable to oppression and whatever else is thrown our way. My aim was to facilitate a story of survival and positive outcomes, not one of vulnerability and deficits.

Clearly, I had a stance that was influenced by my position within the group I had chosen to study. I believed my insider status gave me the right to take that position, but I feared that in taking that position I risked losing credibility as a researcher. My ambivalence was evidenced by my reference to Jamaicans as "they" and not "we" in my presentation. I was torn between my desire to assume the professional identity of "social science researcher" and my responsibility to address those issues I thought were most relevant to my group.

So I had my way and did not make racism the central focus of my study. One of my research goals was to separate the content and effect of immigration-specific stresses from that of general stressful life events. Part of the semistructured interview I conducted involved asking participants to identify those stressful events they had experienced and to assign a stressfulness rating to each stressor before selecting one event to discuss in more detail.

As the interviews progressed, I gradually came to realize I was not the authority on the Jamaican immigrant experience I had thought myself to be. Repeatedly, my respondents told me that the effects of racism *were* an inseparable component of their lives in this predominantly white, urban setting. Sixty percent of the men and women I interviewed reported having experienced discrimination because of their race and rated this as having been a significantly stressful experience for them (a mean stressfulness rating of 3.92 on a 5-point scale). Further, when I asked participants to choose a stressful experience to discuss in more detail, more participants chose to discuss events related to racial discrimination than any other stressor!

I was amazed at the range of their experiences, at the frequency of the occurrences, and at the effect these events had on those who experienced them. I was also humbled to learn how my fairly recent entry to the United States had, in many ways, insulated me from many of the experiences that my participants reported. When I immigrated to the States, I joined an already existing clique of Jamaican-born, upwardly mobile professionals in their late twenties to mid-thirties who lived in the suburbs of New Jersey. I never appreciated how the hurdles my friends had to overcome to get to that point in this country may have affected them. I never asked them, and they never told me. I assumed that although the journey had been (and still was) rough, that Jamaicans simply regarded this as the course they had to take and just did it. I assumed that racism was the problem of those who perpetrated it, that for us it was the proverbial water off the duck's back.

From my participants I learned the apparent successes that immigrants of color achieve are not without costs. Some of these costs are more easily foreseen than others. Having to leave family and friends back home, suffering homesickness, and enduring less than optimal living arrangements are among those stressors immigrants expect to face. However, racism represents a more detrimental stressor that one can never completely prepare for. By its very insidious nature, racial discrimination has the potential to wear away at one's ability to cope, presenting a challenge that requires one to mobilize all vestiges of strength to withstand it or to recover from its effects. And, yes, among those effects for this group is the tendency to reproduce racism not only toward whites, but toward other groups of color.

I learned an important lesson from this unexpected warp in my data. I did find, as I had predicted, that despite the multiple stressors they faced, participants were able to maintain psychological well-being and perceived benefits from having immigrated to the United States. However, what I did not know was *how* my people wanted their story to be told. They saw the difficulties they faced and the benefits they experienced as being inextricably woven. In order to achieve their goals they had to endure hardships, and racism was uppermost among those stressors they experienced and wanted to discuss. To address the fact that they experienced racism did not mean they were victims. In fact, their narratives revealed that they were resilient—strong and resistant. To discount racism as a stressor for this group would be to undervalue their struggle and only tell part of their story. My preoccupation with presenting an account of thriving was preventing me from acknowledging all the dimensions of their experiences, particularly those experiences that were different from mine.

A speed bump of this nature creates a pause for refocusing the research to accommodate the participants' perspective. One challenge for us as researchers is to value unexpected twists in data as alternate paths to discovery. These are not obstacles, but can serve as opportunities to enrich our work and make it more meaningful.

ETHICS COMMITTEES: ON THE DANGERS OF "PROTECTION"

Many speed bumps are biographically induced, as Kenneth Foster and Susan Lombardo reveal. Others are institutionally constructed. The French term for speed bumps translates into "sleeping police," and here—at the site of the Institutional Review Board (IRB)—that translation seems ominously appropriate. Kathleen M. Cumiskey "re-views" her experience with the IRB, the institutional eye for ethics, revealing the ways in which this process is organized, as Brinton Lykes et al. (1996) have argued, to protect the institution rather than our informants. Installed to protect, like those airbags in newer cars, the IRB may—at times—be obscuring, silencing, and not protective for marginalized youth. And yet Cumiskey takes this halting experience as a moment to understand the potential exploitation of research on squatter youth and to broaden the frame around her work from squatter youth to gentrification.

(DE)FACING THE INSTITUTIONAL REVIEW BOARD: WRANGLING THE FEAR AND FANTASY OF ETHICAL DILEMMAS AND RESEARCH ON "AT-RISK" YOUTH

Kathleen M. Cumiskey

In the fall of 1995, I developed a proposal for an ethnography of community and commitment among squatter punk youth in the "East Village"[1] of Manhattan: homeless individuals, ranging in age from 12–24, surviving on their own and living together, communally, in abandoned buildings called "squats." These youth were able to maintain some distance from the social service system and were creating a community and culture to help them meet their basic needs as a group. My methods included participant observation and in-depth interviewing. I had planned to pay each person I interviewed $10. But first I had to confront my university's Institutional Review Board (IRB) and my own ethical apprehensions about what I was proposing to do.

The IRB's response to my proposal came via a letter and from a phone conversation that I had with a committee administrator following the letter. Their concerns spiraled around their assumptions about squatter youth. The committee viewed these young men and women as "youth-at-risk,"[2] in a mode not too dissimilar from Leslie Roman's (1996) analysis of moral panics, in which she argues that when youth are constructed as subjects-at-risk, they also become "subjects of pathology, deviance, and blame and rendered constantly irredeemably alien" (p. 11). They are, then "deserving" of particular paternalistic interventions: "The Committee recommends strongly that you develop and make available to your participants a list of referrals of individuals and agencies that can provide help and services to them."

By making the list of referrals a requirement for approval of my research, the IRB was repositioning me, as well as repositioning the youth. I didn't feel comfortable nor prepared to take on this role. I also believed that if I approached the squatters in this way I would be undermining the goals of my research. They continue:

> The Committee would like you to consider the possibility that the $10 subject fee you will be offering to interviewees could be construed as coercive. Given the poverty of your participants, an offer of cash, even a small amount, might induce some of them to agree to participate only to receive it. Would an offer of a gift certificate, or the purchase of a meal, be possible alternatives? While the value of these other gifts would be comparable to cash, they are less fungible, which would make them less coercive.

Less than clear about what the committee meant by "less fungible," I asked the Assistant Director, who suggested it would be "better for you to hand out McDonald's gift certificates." At least then I "would know where the money was going." Again, the IRB was reconstituting my position with the squatters. "The Committee would like to remind you that the Graduate Center does not indemnify student researchers; if you wish to be indemnified, you must purchase a policy."

The letter went on to indicate the University would not legally represent me, and would withdraw support for my project, in the event that I was arrested or chose to be arrested if my documents were subpoenaed. Now I have to admit that I, myself, may have raised this as a possible concern for my work, yet I never mentioned it in my proposal.

Finally, the Committee wanted:

> A fuller discussion of the risk/benefit ratio of your research. Your discussion should include an assessment of the risk of a breach of confidentiality and anonymity, given the potential for your witnessing illegal activities and police interest in them, and the consequences such a breach would have for your participants. Please explain the benefits your study may have for your participants, if any, and for advancing our understanding of the social world and human behavior. The potential benefits of your research should outweigh the risks involved.

The IRB's response to my project and my own apprehensions made me aware of the risks, and I, too, was beginning to wonder about the benefits to squatters. Herein lies the speed bump. The IRB's response, along with my preliminary observations of media representations of squatters, made me feel as if I had contributed now to the expanded theater in which squatter youths' experiences were being spectacularized. At that point, I returned to the squatter community itself, a community with which I had extensive contact, and ended up "confessing" what I had been doing. I reintroduced myself as a researcher. The squatter youth, once welcoming, were now much more apprehensive. It turned out that their community had been visited frequently by other university students "interested" in their lifestyle as well as newspaper reporters and talk show producers. They felt that their contribution to these sources did nothing to better their living conditions and in fact often attracted negative attention. When asked how could this be prevented, I was provided with an answer that fundamentally altered my project. One squatter responded, "Why do we have to be the subjects?" I flipped. In all of my worry and concern, I never considered shifting the gaze away from scrutinizing these youths' lives. By shifting my focus, I decided to investigate something that affected their lives and the security of their community: the process of gentrification.

Gentrification poses the most serious threat to the extinction of the squatter lifestyle. Gentrification in the "East Village" has been one of the main reasons the squatters have been spectacularized as a deviant group of people trying to inhibit community development. They have been used by developers and politicians as tools to divide neighborhoods and con-stituencies. Yet the squatters themselves have not had much choice in what battles they now face. My research now focuses on how gentrification forces the displacement of most of the long-term residents of the neighborhood, specifically the elderly and lower-income Latino, African American, and white people, and, of course, the squatters (punks, families, and other single persons).

By revealing the impact of gentrification on the people living in the neighborhood, I have uncovered the devastation wrought by corporate and private interests. This, indeed, is the untold story of gentrification. Only at the "speed bump" was I able to question the motives and consequences of my work and "re-view" *which* story had to be told.[3]

PUT ON YOUR HAZARD LIGHTS

Some of us are privileged to work with and for progressive organizations eager to understand "difference" or "conflict" within their internal organi-zational life—school, an AIDS services organization, a church, a battered women's shelter, a youth group that has been informed from clients, staff, students, outsiders, and insiders that there are internal problems operat-ing through gender, race, sexuality, and class. We may be invited in to conduct participatory work and to offer up a fresh look. After much colla-borative work, the air sometimes—not usually, but often—gets thick. The research typically invites a turn from looking at "them"—the "unruly" youth, the "apathetic" parents, the "complaining" clients of color—to an analysis of the organization itself, the institutional contribution to the problem. And with this turn, the research may be resisted in explicit or subtle ways. The report may be deemed erroneous or naive; the gradu-ate students may be seen as too young or inexperienced; the informants may be cast as crying sour grapes; or, preemptively, the interviews and transcriptions may be determined too expensive. Needless to say, we have encountered institutions most welcoming but also those most resistant to the very analyses they commissioned. And we—the couriers—carry the responsibility. As Anne Galletta writes on her personal confrontation with race and class privilege as she conducts ethnographic work in an urban high school, Adrianne Christmas authors her conflicting experi-ences in the black church, and Sean Massey interrogates another instance in which an AIDS services organization, eager to "hear" how clients of color experience the organization, commissions a study and then works hard not to hear.

GETTING MY NAILS DONE

Anne Galletta

I don't usually get my nails done. It's the kind of thing that looks great on others but pretty out of character on me. I didn't want to get them polished, but while I sat interviewing the director of the Center Academy, she asked me would I let one of the students from the nail-brushing class do my nails? I felt a surge of repulsion mix unexpectedly with my eagerness to please the young people and their teachers who were part of a program that had impressed me as having achieved a positive relationship and sense of trust in a building notorious for student alienation, distrust, and despair.

As part of my research on the experience of restructuring in this former comprehensive high school, recently closed and then reopened as a campus of several small new schools, I had spent a good amount of time here as a participant observer. I began the research in the remnant school, the Center Academy, designed to graduate the juniors and seniors of the former comprehensive high school. I was not at all sure how I, a white middle-class graduate student, who lived in a suburb outside the city, with my own children in a suburban public school, would be received by students and teachers in this remnant school.

The principal of the Center Academy encouraged me to spend time with a group of teachers who had fashioned a team structure and re-cruited a group of about 100 students, without regard for academic level or grade point average. The teachers and students were very receptive to my research, and their welcome and openness allayed my fears of es-tablishing trust and credibility. Sometimes, though, I felt an emerging conflict between my desire to reciprocate their welcome and my coming to terms with some critical questions about education and equity. The invitation to get my nails done in a newly established nail-brushing class was indeed such a moment of conflict.

As I climbed the stairs from the first floor to the second, I argued with myself, almost audibly to the stairs littered with candy and junk food wrappers:

> Why am I doing this? A gesture of good will on my part? The teachers—and the kids—are so positive about what's happening here. But what

about this class? What's getting reproduced here? Or is this a harmless diversion for students in this phase-out school, a place where students tell me they feel safe, where they enjoy learning.

But, I don't want to get my nails polished. I don't want to sit there and act like isn't this great. How can they study algebra or biology when they're taking a class on nail brushing?

"Great—came to get your nails done?" From a group of Latino and African American young women, the teachers called over Patricia, who was African American. We introduced ourselves and settled into two desks that faced each other.

Though I knew a number of the students from my visits to this school already, I had not seen Patricia before. Like many of the students here, she seemed older. She was friendly and at ease chatting. She wore a felt hat that lay softly on top of her head. On her desk she had a bottle of rubbing alcohol, a handful of cotton balls, several small plastic tools, and some bottles of polish. She took my hands, which lay limp in hers, and fell into a comfortable silence while she began to work on my nails. I sat in a quiet that seemed much too loud to me.

I tried to tell myself to just relax and participate in an activity that everybody else in the room seemed to be enjoying. I wanted to pay attention, to catch the conversations, observe the interactions, imprint the experience in my mind for later fieldnotes. But the quiet between Patricia and me seemed like an enormous void that I wanted in some way to fill.

It wasn't only my awkwardness about getting my nails done. Nor was it my ambivalence over the dubious educational purpose of this class. It was the physical presence of this young woman, African American, tending to my hands, my fingers. As Patricia rubbed them with alcohol, my whiteness became as perceptibly strong to me as the scent of the alcohol smarting my nose, and I felt an overwhelming desire to run as far away from this place as I could. Suddenly everything about my white, middle-class background, which I had sought to mask in my fieldwork in this school, tumbled out and landed loudly, cluttering up the space between us.

In an effort to put myself more at ease, I struck up a conversation with Patricia, which began more like a structured interview and then unfolded into a chat. Patricia told me (I asked her) that she had been in the program since March, and she planned to graduate from Center this June. She lived near the school but had avoided it in ninth grade because of its bad reputation. She told me her mother wrote many letters to keep her out of Center. In the end she did well on the admission test at Stuyvesant, a very selective and competitive public high school, and was accepted there. She left after a year to have her son.

Willie, a Latino teacher I had interviewed earlier whom I also observed teaching a drama class where the students did spontaneous scripts about relationship and conflict, leaned over my shoulder and said, "Thanks for being a guinea pig." I told him it was a great freebie and I didn't mind being a guinea pig at all. As a matter of fact, I told him, I had also consented to a haircut in the future.

> See, they recognize my willingness to jump in and be a part of the work they are trying to accomplish here. It feels good to know they see me as supportive. But what is the work they are trying to accomplish? What is it that I'm playing a part in?
>
> Participant observation means being a part of what's going on, right? But what if what's going on is something you're uncomfortable with? Where does this discomfort come from? Is it a cultural artifact? Or is it something else. . . . And what do I do with it?
>
> What does participation really mean? Collusion? Interruption? Or something else?
>
> After Patricia applied the final coat of clear polish on top of the soft pink, I felt the confusion rush in again. I wanted to praise her work, and indeed it looked good, but at the same time I felt I wanted to duck into the nearest bathroom and wash it all off, wash the memory of this uncomfortable moment, the confrontation of my privileged race and class, and the discomfort I felt in being an accomplice in displacing academics and reinforcing particular narrow, stereotypical career options for the young women in this school.
>
> This course—it's the irritant I want to scratch away, it's the nagging awareness of our race and class difference, and the institution of schooling's response to that difference: white is privileged; brown and black are not. It doesn't feel right, my being a part of this; now I'm part of the machinery, implicit or not, that sanctions disparate educational outcomes based on class and color. Would I endorse this course of study to my daughters? No.

Why does this experience haunt me so? Every time I look at my fingernails my immediate distaste for the light pink against my white skin throws me into a state of confusion as I try to reconcile the warmth and calm in that classroom, the pleasure the students showed toward their work, Patricia's absorption as she walked down the hall crocheting, my outrage over the fact that more was not happening for these students and that I, too, had been an accomplice in this setup. In my confusion it is hard to pry apart the different threads of good intentions, racism, the influence of poverty, the effects of institutional reform that changes everything but transforms nothing (Fine, 1992), and the history of neglect on the part of the school system toward the young people in this community:

> Parents' comments at the last parent association meeting: "These kids have been so disrespected by the system," says a parent, "now my kid likes coming to school. He talks about school all the time." Another parent says, "It's good, what I see happening for my daughter. But *I* need to ask about her math, is she getting what she needs to graduate?"

As I write, already more than a year has passed since I drafted these fieldnotes. Patricia finished her year at Center Academy, graduated, and went to work. Her hopes of attending a technical college fell through when she found that she couldn't financially support her son and herself as a college student. Furthermore, she learned the September after graduation that her high school diploma was revoked, due to the school system's dissatisfaction with the Center Academy's academic program, its firing of the principal, and accusations by the system that the school did not provide students with adequate academic instruction for the credits given. The school system's actions created a sense of vindication among some educators and community members, and a chilling effect among others. Many of the students and their parents felt, once again, betrayed; some felt the decision was justified. Either way, an academic year was lost, and, for some, the chance to secure a high school degree will never happen.

I am still muddling through questions from my research in this remnant school, questions about education and equity, questions about research methodology. How do schools better serve African American and Latino youth in poor communities without reproducing gender, race, and class inequities? When am I as researcher, often a participant/participant observer, often in public schools in poor communities, helping reproduce inequitable practices and policies? And understanding the ease with which my research can become an act of collusion, I find myself asking, what does productive, critical interruption look like?

INSIDER/OUTSIDER:
ON WHAT SIDE OF THE SIDEWALK DOES YOUR SHADOW FALL?

Adrianne Christmas

Before the start of informal/formal interviews, as well as during participant observations, I was questioned. "Are you saved?" "Do you believe
in the Lord Jesus Christ?" "Sister, have you accepted Jesus Christ as your
personal Lord and Savior?" Feeling interrogated by the "Spiritual Police,"
there were times I wanted to plead the Fifth Amendment or have a com-
petent lawyer present. But such incidents did not stop me. My image cast
a tall, lean, and strong shadow on the right side of the sidewalk with the
sun at my back. This was good, like a warm feeling of support from God
that I was doing okay in collecting the data. However, when the sun
shifted, I became blinded by its rays. My shadow no longer was to the
right—it was on the left, behind me, or just not there. This is where the
blinding rays of racial identity and narrow demands of loyalty caused
my shadow to become short, distorted, somewhere behind me, or gone
altogether.

As an African American female, I know who and what I am better than
anyone else. So when the questions of, "How black are you?" were raised
because of my affiliation with a predominantly white institution, I was
prepared with a plan of attack. But what I was not prepared for was their
counterattack of blocking the sun from my eyes and causing my shadow
to shift and disappear. "Who are you to air to those white people what goes
on over here?" This I did not expect from my *own* people, who encourage
any educational pursuits regardless of which university/college an African
American attended. I had run into a brick wall and my strong, lean, and
tall shadow was gone.

Throughout my educational pursuits, I have had the "blessings" of
many African Americans in the Buffalo community. Their "blessings"
included moral and sometimes economic support, if not the rigorous
questioning as to how I was doing in school and why I wasn't someplace
writing/reading papers. They were the motivator in my life when I felt I
had run out of steam to move forward. It is as if I was not only getting this
degree for myself, but for the entire African American race. But this was
before the study began. People at my research site were happy that I was
working toward a Ph.D. until they discovered they were the subjects of the
study. Some have called me at home as well as at the university to see if I
had completed the "book" and to see if I needed anything. Other people

changed by avoiding me or telling their friends to "watch out" for me. What in the world am I to do now?

We never talked about such issues in the qualitative research courses. Will my non-African American adviser understand what I am talking about and the pain I feel? Am I really displaying the "dirty laundry" of one black community in Buffalo? But what about my pledge of dedication, my mission and goals for real social change (self-empowerment) for the communities (and people) to which I have a connection? Am I a traitor to the black race and will I possibly become labeled as a "Judas" among my own people? Will this circulate through the church and bias the people I want to interview? Would I be able to get *any* interviews? Will the participants be themselves and speak freely as opposed to telling me what they think I want to hear? This is a black church community where the ministers have continuous interaction with each other and various congregations across the country. Will they warn other black churches about me?

My misery came from taking a Bible study course on Marriage and the Black Family. Much of what I had witnessed in this class gave me second thoughts about getting married. My role as the female was described in a very demeaning way. I was subordinate in relation to my husband. Women in the class, who were not much older than I, had stated that they wanted to have someone dominant over them, "a man that would take control and run things." As a strong, independent African American woman, instead of feeling as if I were in class, I felt as if I had gotten stuck in a time warp dating 1950. Sitting in this class was not the difficult part. Keeping silent about how I felt when asked by the instructor was one of the most difficult tasks.

Throughout this project, I had to refocus and change my attack in getting people to talk with me candidly about their experiences. I had, for example, to constantly reassure them that I was not an FBI agent sent to close down the church. As it turns out, members of the church were under federal investigation for what will remain an undisclosed matter. All of this surfaced after "bumping" into a friend of mine who is an FBI agent one day while I was entering the research site. Not only was I questioned by the congregationalists, my so-called friend took liberty in questioning me in the main parking lot in front of the main entrance to the church during the weekday in front of congregation members. There were telephone calls to university administrators questioning my status as a student as opposed to what they assumed me to be—an FBI agent. (Believe me, I was contacted by the FBI as to why they were receiving calls from a local black church about me being an agent.) This is something I would expect to see on television, or happening to someone else in the field. I repeatedly had to say to myself, "All I want is to complete the degree requirements and get a job. Is that asking too much?" Apparently so, if such requirements instill fear among African American congregational members that I will "expose" their "issues" to those outside of their community.

I have been in contact with numerous African American professors and administrators across the country who have been positioned as outsiders by their own racial or ethnic groups throughout their research experiences. Their advice to me: Hang in there, follow your conscience, remain true to yourself, keep your head held high, and never burn the bridges that you have crossed.

CRITICAL IMPLICATIONS OF THE MUNDANE

Sean Massey

As a graduate student who frequently utilizes qualitative methods and who approaches social psychological issues from a qualitative stance (Kidder & Fine, 1997), I've been warned of the influence that relations of power can have on the design and implementation of the research project. In the past, I have chosen qualitative methodologies because they more readily forefront the voices of those traditionally kept silent in social science research (Ladner, 1971). I have come to realize, however, that making voices heard is not the final step in the qualitative project. There must also be those willing to listen. I write on a project which "carried" the voices of institutional critique that few wanted to hear.

I was working as a research associate in an evaluation unit of a large AIDS services organization which served an increasingly diverse client population of people with AIDS. In the recent past, an organized group of board members, clients, and staff had publicly criticized the organization, charging that it was racist and sexist. Management responded to these claims with a commitment to investigate, asking the evaluation unit to conduct a research project to assess clients' overall satisfaction with agency services and, more specifically, their experiences of discrimination, their perceptions of the multicultural atmosphere of the organization and of the sensitivity with which services had been delivered.

As a result, a rather extensive phone survey was conducted, complemented by a series of focus groups designed to elicit the opinions of a wide range of client groups—gay white men, straight black women, lesbian and bisexual women, Latino gay men (in Spanish and in English), and so forth. Management envisioned a small qualitative component to this project but expressed a greater urgency to quantify the magnitude of the problem. My supervisor and I were both aware, however, of the importance of qualitative data in assessing perceptions of and experiences with racial and gender bias (Kincheloe & McLaren, 1994). Through our insistence, the focus groups received equal attention in the research process. In the end over 600 clients were interviewed for the survey and 12 different focus groups were conducted (with an average of 10 clients each). What follows is a discussion of three "bumps" we encountered as this project progressed and as we attempted to maintain a qualitative component.

Bump 1. The problem centered around the unwillingness on the part of the managing director to allocate the money necessary to have all the tapes sent out to "professional" transcribers.[4] The per-page costs of transcription were prohibitive. Fortunately, we were able to recruit transcribers from the large pool of agency volunteers, including several bilingual volunteers for the focus groups conducted in Spanish. With a little training, the volunteers, all of whom had typing skills and had expressed interest in the job, were brought up to speed on the basics of transcription techniques and formatting. Each volunteer did approximately two- to three-hour shifts, at the end of which they often wandered away in the transcendental daze that can come about from the intense concentration required for transcription. First problem resolved.

Bump 2. One particular event several weeks into the transcription phase led me to confront my taken-for-granted attitude toward the transcription phase of the study. A straight white woman volunteer, whom we considered one of the best transcribers, was sitting at a workstation transcribing a tape from what would be the third or fourth focus group she had completed. As she proceeded, she was becoming increasingly agitated—she typed, replayed the tape, typed some more, became more agitated, replayed the tape, and so on. As I approached her desk, I heard her mumbling, "I can't stand this . . . I don't understand these women . . . they aren't speaking clearly."

The tape was from the focus group of heterosexual black women, the clients we suspected were most "in need" of any interviewed. They needed not only the services currently being offered, such as support groups, they also needed child care, activities and services where their spouses and children could join them for activities, and services closer to their homes or transportation assistance. Their problems stemmed not only from difficulties typically associated with an AIDS diagnosis, but included problems related to class, race, and gender bias, as well as issues related to their being heterosexual in a traditionally gay organization. The group most demographically different from our modal client—white gay men—and probably most alienated from the organization "couldn't be understood."

Why was this tape so difficult to transcribe? The reason the volunteer gave was that "the women were difficult to understand," that they "weren't speaking clearly." One conclusion is that the tape was difficult because focus groups are notoriously difficult to transcribe. In addition, this group of women were engaged in a "call and response" kind of discussion, where one woman would narrate an experience and several others would voice encouragement or express understanding or empathy at the same time she was speaking. Further, some of the women were of Caribbean descent and spoke with accents that this volunteer may have been unfamiliar with. This volunteer, however, had transcribed several other focus groups, including members from different ethnic groups, with different dialects and conversational patterns. Thus, we resisted a cultural explanation.

Another explanation is tied to this volunteer's connection to the organization. In the past most of the agency's clients had been white gay men. The services of the organization were explicitly organized around the needs of this constituency. This focus group involved *women*, not men, who were *heterosexual*, not homosexual and *black*, not white. Their conversation may not have "fit" the volunteer's understanding or expectations of typical client needs.

At this point, I have no way of teasing apart the "real" reasons why this volunteer was unable to transcribe this tape. Motive, however, is not always the point—potential consequences for research and policy should be. A group of women, marginalized within this context and in desperate need of services, were at risk for not getting the "air time" they needed to voice their concerns about organizational practice.

Bump 3 and a Flat Tire. Whatever the volunteer's motivation for not finishing the tape, this experience served as a metaphor for the relationship between the AIDS organization and the project. From the beginning it was clear that the organization wasn't very interested in the data from the focus groups. This was an organization undergoing incredible change, provoking profound organizational decisions given its growing awareness of the demographic breadth of the AIDS epidemic. Should the organization maintain its historic commitment toward the group who originally founded the organization and were originally being served by the organization—gay white men? Or, should commitments be widened to embrace those now targeted by the epidemic—lesbians, heterosexual women and men, people of color, IV drug users, and the poor? This institutional ambivalence became silent in the agency's concerns around choice of method, project costs, and in the production of the final report.

As the project neared its end, there was a push to "get out" the survey data as quickly as possible. As is typical of satisfaction surveys in general (especially those conducted in a health care setting), the numeric results skew in a positive direction, indicating an overwhelmingly favorable view of agency service. With a great deal of technical and political effort, we disaggregated the numbers demonstrating among other things that nonwhite clients had reported experiencing more discrimination, which may have led to their also reporting more negative assessments of the multicultural atmosphere and less satisfaction with overall agency services.

As expected, however, the most compelling and nuanced criticisms, as well as suggestions for improvement, were found in the focus-group material. These groups provided a forum for clients to corroborate experiences. Many clients, in a leap of faith, took this opportunity to both critique and offer suggestions for improvement. Eventually, a report of the focus-group data was written and submitted to the executive director. As of today, however, both reports have been filed somewhere. No new programs, or program enhancements, have resulted from the study.

Qualitative researchers may collect data in such a way as to illuminate the textured experiences and analyses of participants. We may be able to bring forward stories that reveal hidden challenges, which remain hidden in more cursory methods. What is not guaranteed by method, however, is that our audiences will be able and/or willing to hear these stories once analyzed. This speed-bump tale is meant not as an indictment of the organization nor of the volunteer. I simply ask that we always question the relations of power as they determine the questions we do (and don't) ask, and also how we ask, analyze, and listen to the answers we are given.

THEORIZING SILENCES, ERASURES, WHAT IS NOT SAID

Across our works, we recognize that narratives do not, can not, should not be seen as speaking for themselves. We know, of course, that theory profoundly informs our work. And yet, in our projects we have been pressed beyond what we knew, pressed to consider how to theorize social histories of informants, the relations of narrative coconstruction, what is said and what is not, what is visible and what has been erased. Rosemarie A. Roberts, Juan G. Valentin-Juarbe, and Susan Weseen join British theorist Mik Billig (1994) and U.S. developmentalist Deborah Tolman (1994) in trying to develop a language for theorizing the interview relation—the interruptions, silences, gaps, spaces, and hesitations. Knowing that narratives provide a partial opening for social inquiry, these three struggle with how to theorize narrative production as it shapes and mutates the very material we cocollect.

MUERTOS: THE DEAD SIGNAL US TO REMEMBER

Rosemarie A. Roberts

My husband and I decided to return to our parents' soil to be married. After weighing our options between Nevis, Florida, Puerto Rico, or Cuba, we settled on Puerto Rico.

The day after the ceremony we drove from the mountains, along the eastern coast to the Caribbean Sea. "And on your way there, you must stop at *The Resort*. They have one of the best snorkeling spots." So we were told by a native. With map in hand, we got out early in the morning. I white-knuckled it on narrow winding mountain roads, swearing the car wouldn't fit on the road (I should have gotten a minicompact) as cars careened around the bend in the opposite direction. Once I got used to it and the circulation in my hands returned, I could bask in my childhood memories of the Puerto Rican countryside I love: the brightly painted concrete houses with *abuelo y abuela* on the front porch, the cows in the pasture, and the chickens and goats in the road. The mountain road suddenly opens on the *autopisto*, or highway, and the signs of *The Resort* loom large in the horizon.

After two guard stops, we are directed to a cookie-cutter island resort with terra-cotta tiled floors, strategically located palm trees, and bellboys in tropical-print shirts and white shorts, socks, and shoes. Standing at the desk, I await my turn amongst lobster-red tourists in big hats and white tube socks. I'm directed away from the hotel, deeper into the resort by the friendly bilingual concierge, who insists on speaking English while I insist on speaking Spanish. Back in the car, we drive through a pristine, every-house-looks-the-same housing development, miss our turn and we're lost. We stop a friendly looking guy in a golf cart, wearing a tropical print shirt, who turns out to be a real estate agent. "Take the first left and after two *muertos* take a right," says the real estate agent with the shark-like smile. His voice, a distant sound in the background, as my mind wraps around the "two *muertos*." I shoot my husband a panicked side glance and pray he's paying attention to the directions. I'm stuck on the *muertos* which means "the dead" in Spanish. Why is the real estate agent so nonchalantly telling me to drive over two dead people in the road, I wonder. Then it hits me. He's talking about "speed bumps." Yes, of course, dead bodies in the road would make you slow down or stop dead in your tracks.

What a wonderful metaphor for my work. The dead stop me. They make me slow down to notice them, to notice their/our buried past and absent legacy, the legacy we are so often forced to forget in the neocolonial Americas. I look around me and try to imagine how many people had to give up their homes and their livelihoods for the sake of the sprawling *expensive* development? Where are the *abuelos y abuelas*, the keepers of history tucked in the folds of their aging skin and the tears that collect around their eyes as they reminisce about the way it was?

As we are reminded by Billig (1995), while American citizens shake their fingers at those outsider nationalists in "foreign" places, we miss

> the little ways the citizenry are daily reminded of the national place in the world of nations. However, this reminding is so familiar, so continual, that it is not consciously registered as reminding. The metonymic image of banal nationalism is not a flag which is being waved with fervent passion; it is a flag hanging unnoticed in the public building. (p. 8)

In a world built on unequal power relations, marginalized communities based on class, race/ethnicity, and gender have to struggle to maintain/ sustain/remember their identity, "the embodied habits of social life" (p. 8) and their culture. Erika Apfelbaum (1979) makes clear that within unequal power relations, the dominating force "relies on procedures such as the destruction of cultural heritage, combined with the disappearance of the [marginalized] community's traditions and its own ways and means for expressing them" (p. 200). Apfelbaum continues:

> The outcome of . . . historical and cultural genocide, whether by active policy or by omission, legitimizes the domination and, in robbing the (group) of its internal supports, guarantees the dependency and the impotence of the sub-ordinated (group) and the marginality of its members. (p. 201)

Recently I undertook a study of a contested spiritual community in the United States. I was interested in looking at the intragroup dynamics, specifically how the community maintains connectedness through instances of conflict and difference. My inquiry led me not only to the inside borders of the community, but also to look at historical mainstream cultural hegemonic pressures on community borders and their influences on in-group dynamics. As Fine and Weis (1996) point out, interview participants are not always adept at narrating the social forces that interrupt/suppress or oppress them, or in the case of my study, attempt to erase their history, traditions, and cultural identity. Like *The Resort* sign, they are written over. The looming question for me is how can I understand what occurs today in a contested spirited community, without documenting the historical attempt at "cultural genocide"? Interviews of community members would not be enough. And yet it is often difficult to study empirically (even in qualitative research) the mechanisms of power used by dominating groups to rob a group of their history and traditions (see Allport, 1942; Espin, 1994; Nagata, 1990; Stewart, Franz, & Layton, 1988). Thus, I added historic archival research of a major court challenge to the community.

Only through history could I determine how mechanisms of power were deployed against remembering. Hurtado and Stewart (1997) remind us that studying different power positions require different methods. *The Resort*, in all its colonial splendor, and the lack of diversity, cemeteries, or markers of the past, yelled so loudly about what is missing when we focus only on what is visible. Driving over the *muertos* we must remember social forces designed to maintain dominant standards and to suppress, raze, forget, erase, and silence dominant cultures and histories.

"EL PROBLEMA DEL CUAL NO PUEDO HABLAR" (THE PROBLEM ABOUT WHICH I CANNOT SPEAK)

Juan G. Valentin-Juarbe

Carmen is the mother of a couple of my students at the urban school where I've worked as an English as a Second Language teacher for the last three years. I've known her that long. Being the only Spanish-speaking teacher there—and Puerto Rican—I double as social worker, counselor, and community liaison. Last year the daughter, Lidia, who was 15 then, ran away from home. Carmen would come to my classroom and tell me—in tears—her ordeal. For weeks, Carmen didn't know where her daughter was. She became a sort of detective in her despairing search for her daughter. She would narrate to me how day after day she would get in her car and rummage the West Side of Buffalo looking for Lidia. Risking her life, she would go into apartments where she thought Lidia might be. I could see Carmen deteriorate both physically and emotionally.

Eventually, Lidia turned up in Dunkirk, New York, a town about 50 miles south of Buffalo. How Carmen found her, I don't know. She was living with a 34-year-old man who has six children (not with her), the oldest of whom is a 12-year-old daughter. Since Lidia had left school, Child Abuse came into the picture to investigate possible neglect, and Carmen got scared. This year Lidia turned 16 and, with Carmen's consent, married Joel, Lidia's beloved.

Now her sons have become jealous of Lidia and have turned against their mother. "How come she can get married and we can't even bring a girl home?" they ask her (they are 17 and 13). She has recently told me these sons want her out of the house because she is "not needed." They want her to go live with Lidia. Over the phone, the night she told me this story, she also told me how she hadn't cooked for the boys that evening. The next day, her son Alberto had a stomach ache at school and was accusing Carmen of neglect. "If she's not gonna cook for us, she better go," he declared.

Now Carmen confesses she curses the day she came to the United States. Her kids never wanted to come here and blame her, as she blames herself, for their unhappiness. Alberto's art project for school is a drawing of the American and Puerto Rican flags fused together with a plane coming from Puerto Rico to the United States. In the foreground there is a boy surrounded by flames. It depicts his rage; *he* is in flames because of the uprooting.

Since Carmen has spoken openly to me before, I thought she would have no apprehension when talking about her problem on tape. When she referred to Lidia during the interview, she called it "the problem about which I cannot speak." My heart stopped. She claims Child Abuse began to investigate her after she spoke openly in a session with a social worker from a government agency.

Before the interview began, I sat at her kitchen table and we conversed while Carmen cooked dinner for her sons and me. Then, she spoke passionately about her worries and troubles. The same happened after the tape recorder was off and we were just talking in her living room. On tape, however, there is little evidence of this woman's desperation.

After the interview, I was not only disappointed but also found myself in a dilemma. Like Rosemarie Roberts's *muertos*, this woman chose *not* to expose a piece of her history. How do I respect this decision? What do I do with the information I know and which she left out? How do I convey her desperation? Off tape, she tells me she's losing her mind over Lidia. On tape, she doesn't even mention her. But then again, why should I probe more to get "juicy" data, when I can see Carmen falling apart in front of my eyes?

INTERVIEWING NEW MOTHERS

Susan Weseen

"Women have always lied to each other."
"Women have always whispered the truth to each other."
Both of these axioms are true.
—Adrienne Rich

The tape recorder lay abandoned in a room near the attic—the scene of the last of several unsuccessful attempts at an interview earlier that afternoon. Coming downstairs from putting my daughter to sleep, I saw Laura alone in the kitchen, still working while everyone else watched television several rooms away. Her seven-month-old son was sleeping, after having cried himself to sleep—20 long minutes of crying. Finally without children to worry about, I took a deep breath and said something about how exhausting the work of motherhood could be. Laura sighed too and, almost as if to ward off any ideas I might have had about trying to start "The Interview" yet again, apologized for being so tired, saying that she was going to do a few more dishes and then go to bed.

Her instincts were right: I had wanted to try again. My daughter and I were leaving the next morning after a short Passover visit with my friend and her family, and this was the last chance we would have to talk about her experience as a new mother for my study of the transition to motherhood. But my determination to make one last attempt came more out of a sense of obligation and looming deadlines than real eagerness. The first few times we had tried to speak "officially," it had felt exactly like all the other interviews I had done thus far: remarkably flat and frustrating. It was almost as though both the women with whom I spoke and I myself were skating around the real story, talking niceties which neither of us believed, but which we all refused to jettison.

Despite Laura's announcement of fatigue, it was only one seemingly insignificant comment later, with the tape recorder safely out of reach two floors above, that Laura and I suddenly found ourselves deeply immersed in what turned out to be a two-hour-long conversation that opened up into a whole range of admissions and revelations about her conflicted feelings of being a mother. I was stunned; where had this come from? And why now? She spoke quickly, urgently, and quietly. Even though we were far out of earshot of the rest of the household, I had to lean forward and concentrate hard just to hear her. As story after story rolled out, I cursed the tape recorder's absence. In furtive glances around the room, I saw that pencils or paper were similarly missing. Realizing that the world had conspired to keep the props of a researcher out of my hands, I tried to give myself up to an astoundingly detailed account of the silenced aspects of motherhood, praying that my memory would hold at least some of her words.

But I couldn't hold out. Once, when Laura excused herself to say good night to her husband before he went to sleep, I bolted out of the kitchen and raced to retrieve the tape recorder. Seconds later, I heard her footsteps heading toward the stairs. Not wanting her to return to an empty table, I quickly reversed direction and stumbled back downstairs. A few minutes later, as she was about to launch into a description of just what it was that has made mothering so hard for her, I bit my tongue quickly, but could not stop myself from asking her for some paper. I held my breath with worry for the two long minutes it took her to find a scrap of junk mail and a dull pencil, but when she sat back down, she didn't miss a beat. Barely looking up while I scribbled furiously, I apologized for the lack of eye contact. She quickly dismissed the apology, saying that our conversation felt like a meeting of the mother's group she had never been able to persuade anyone else to join.

Finally, half an hour into the "interview," Laura's sister came in to wash some dishes during a commercial break. I hesitated for a moment, but then excused myself and leapt up the stairs three at a time to get the tape recorder. It was just too hard to take notes and concentrate, and I was losing half of what she was saying, anyway. Although I worried that the presence of the tape recorder would alter the depth and flow of our conversation, I took the risk. My apprehension was unwarranted. Instead, she was so eager to continue her train of thought that she barely noticed me setting up the recorder. Finally, everything I want in an interview: what feels like deep, honest communication and a tape recorder "getting it all down" (see Massey earlier in this chapter, about what transcriptions miss) so that it is "sanctioned" data.

Although this encounter with Laura was perhaps the most vivid example of my participants' reluctance to go "on the record" about the difficult aspects of mothering, it was not an isolated case. It seems that the mothers I have interviewed—or attempted to interview—are already deeply aware that, as writer Nina Barrett (1994) suggests, motherhood has a "rambling, incoherent drone that drives away bystanders." If you have the experience of speaking—or trying to speak—about something that "drives people away," you learn not to talk about it. Or, like Jane (another new mother with whom I spoke), you talk about it in a blurred rush in an elevator as you trail the interviewer out of your home, after the official interview is over, after the tape recorder is turned off, after the interviewer becomes a real person and opens the door with a password of sorts—an admission of her own that challenges the taboos around the difficult aspects of mothering. Or, as Phoebe did, you might try to ignore the constant welling up of tears throughout the interview, in which you say that everything is unbelievably fine and happy. Or you end up like Laura, surprised and pleased and a little hesitant to find herself in the position of being asked to talk about motherhood, but still not willing to go deep until late at night, sitting at the kitchen table, the two of us alone.

In my work with new mothers, I keep feeling that I am also interviewing what Virginia Woolf (1921/1944) has termed the angel in the house. In describing this angel, Woolf writes:

> She was intensively sympathetic. She was immensely charming. She was utterly unselfish. She sacrificed herself daily. If there was a chicken, she took the leg; if there was a draught, she sat in it—in short, she was so constituted that she never had a mind of her own or a wish of her own, but preferred always to sympathize with the minds and wishes of others. . . . She slipped behind me and whispered . . . "Be sympathetic; be tender; flatter; deceive; use all the wiles of our sex." (pp. 58–59)

In my interviews, this angel's presence is hard to pin down, although she leaves traces everywhere. She keeps slipping through my fingers—a glimpse and then she's gone. And somehow it feels as if she is never explicitly present, except in my analysis. I struggle with the dilemma of how to make visible the work of the erasure—how to theorize the denied. How do I presume the presence and content of what Magda Lewis (1993) terms "dangerous memories"—what women might say if they were free of the angel's dictates?

But I also struggle with the angel's presence in my life and work. Her voice tells me that I need to be a neutral presence during the interview, that I can't share my responses with participants, that a friend is not an appropriate "research subject." She also orchestrates the shifts and silences I impose throughout the interview, despite my best efforts to remain a "neutral" presence. During focus groups, she is in my throat as I panic in fear at an interminably long pause before someone answers one of my questions, as I steer away from asking blunt questions about the difficult aspects of motherhood in a desire to maintain the illusion that we—a group of new mothers, some of us with babies, some of us not—are simply gathered to have a couple of hours together on a sunny patch of grass away from what they all described at one point or another as their "confining houses."

Michelle Fine and Susan Merle Gordon (1992) write that "women's unpaid work includes collecting, retaining, and *never revealing* social secrets about men's and women's lives; about oppressive social and economic arrangements and the ideologies that make it 'go down easier'" (p. 20). As the mother of a young child, surrounded by friends who are also mothers, I am certain that motherhood as an institution is built on a foundation of social secrets, as Juan Valentin-Juarbe's analysis suggests. But I am learning that it isn't so easy to document the presence of an absence. When the context of the talk shifts from playgrounds and kitchens and phone calls to tape recorders, and the purpose of the talk shifts from commiseration to documentation, suddenly we all are struck dumb. Until, that is, we manage to sidle into those private crevices in which secrets can be told again.

IN WHOSE VOICE SHALL I WRITE?

In the academy, faculty are pressed—and so we pressure students—to write with multiple voices. Clearly there is a correct one—the academic voice— and yet we and others have nudged our students to write in multiple discourses, in scholarly costumes, in accessible community talk, in policy language. In the next section Jennifer Ayala invites us to consider how the same project "reads" across dialects; and Sarah Carney invites us into the contradictory discourses surrounding the bodies of skaters. Then Corrine Bertram explores the starts and stutters of women as they narrate abuse at the hands of their families.

ACROSS DIALECTS

Jennifer Ayala

In this piece I present an interpretation of narrative material in three different voices. I self-consciously deploy different lenses for interpreting these materials and (re)presenting my work. Borrowing from Laurel Richardson's invitation to produce "writing-stories," these three reveal very different genres but also allegiances and commitments. The first segment is narrated in the voice of "science," perhaps most suitable for a traditional social psychology article. The second voice speaks through standpoint theory, where I position myself as a Latino researcher whose interpretations stem from theory and biography. The third way I write this is in the form of a poem, moving between mothers' and daughters' voices, at times blurring the distinction by making their words intersect. Writing this poem is itself an interpretation, as I use many of the words respondents have used and combine them to form a particular story.

Se habla Academy-Speak

Social learning theorists (e.g., Bandura, 1977) posit that the mechanism through which socialization takes place is observational learning, whereby children learn by observing models, such as parents, perform behaviors and receive reinforcement. This theory presumes that the process of socialization is unidirectional, as children observe parents, learn from them, and act accordingly. The present study questions the unidirectionality of socialization and posits that this process is a bidirectional one.

Preliminary results from this study suggest that the cultural socialization of Latinas across generations does not simply involve adolescents modeling or mimicking adults. Instead, daughters described witnessing the consistencies and inconsistencies in what their mothers said and what they did, and learning from this *discrepancy*. Instead of simply modeling after their mothers, they revisited or attempted to resolve in raising their daughters sets of issues they found important when they were raised. In the interviews, when asked what daughters have taught their mothers, all had responded by describing the ways in which mothers respect their daughters. Mutual respect was a common theme across the interviews when describing the process of socialization. The process of socialization among Latino mothers and daughters may be one of shared, sometimes contentious, respect. The descriptor *shared* is key here, as it implies a reciprocality in the Latino mother-daughter relationship that is often not recognized in the current social learning literature.

Voicing My Position(ality)

I write as a Latina, embodying what Hidalgo (1998) calls an "overlapping insider/outsider status." This affects how I interview, what I find, how I interpret what I find. An insider to the community of respondents I am interviewing, I share Latino cultural citizenship (Flores & Benmayor, 1997), and I live in the same neighborhood as most of my respondents. My outsider status stems from the stretch of our educational, national, and generational differences. As I speak with Latino girls and mothers, I find that I sit between generations; I could be the older sister or *madrina* of the girls and the daughter or younger sister of some of the mothers.

While I recognize my overlapping insider/outsider status, I do not always trust my insider knowledge/theories. Sometimes I "forget" I even have it, caught up as I am in the "ways of the researcher"—the "ways" which tell us again and again that insider knowledge (or any knowledge outside the academy) is not valid or legitimate. For example, when I began interviewing, I was (pleasantly) surprised to find that asking respondents to articulate the ways in which daughters have taught their mothers in the context of the mother-daughter relationship, did not elicit the puzzling looks and hesitant responses I somewhat expected. As I went through the transcripts more carefully, I noticed that the girls and women responded to this question by talking about the qualities daughters had that their mothers did not, but wish they had. My initial interpretation was that respondents did not understand the question in the way that I intended and so I concluded that my wording of the question was at fault. This may be true; however, my adviser helped me reframe this question by pointing out that respondents were talking about the ways in which mothers respected daughters. Of course! *Respeto*. The cross-generational process of transmitting values surrounding culture and gender among Latinas probably involves a shared respect, revealing the reciprocality between mother and daughter, as culture is carried through veins of *respeto*. This interpretation rings true to my insider experiences, which I sometimes suspended. Why did I not see this sooner?

Pressed to conform to the social science mandates of objectivity and neutrality, I (like other researchers) have learned too adeptly to suppress my insider knowledges. We may be told this knowledge is not "true" or "legitimate" or we may tell ourselves this same fiction. Now that opportunities are beginning to arise where some faculty encourage us to expand, draw upon our own personal funds of knowledge and be creative, it is difficult—I find it difficult at times—to come out of the tidy boxes I/we have been crouched in for so long and reach back to remember my/our insider knowledge.

In the vo(I)ces of *madre* and *hija*

> *Mi mami es muy fuerte de caracter*
> in a way that I never could be . . .
> but perhaps I am.
> I can also be *fuerte de caracter.*
> I am also *determinante.*

When I came from *allá*
I was my own mother,
I was my own body.
I had freedom
But with great responsibility.
I could not say
I'm tired,
No puedo trabajar.
But I always heard
mami's voice
echoing in my soul.
And *mijita*,
I try to tell you my struggles
para que aprendas,
so you could learn
from me.

I saw strength in your moments of
weakness
read defiance when you mouthed
fear
And saw a wolf.
Even when *papi*
Wouldn't see what you have inside.
You may not always tell me your
stories in words,
but I can hear them in your tears,
as you carry culture
in your words
in your silences
in your tears
in your prayers.
And I bear witness to your actions.
Yes *mami*, I hear your words
but the music is louder.
And I learn from your contradictions.

Together we weave a fabric of culture
With threads of *respeto* and love.

Y como mama
I want to keep you close to me

Y como hija,
I will try to

but also let you grow.
I will give you *confianza*
and tell you how it is
how I see it
in a way that my *mami* never did,
though I hear her echoes in my soul,

Push the boundary outward.
Find the limit you set
and press it further,
challenge you,
even though it may hurt you
As you did with your *mami*

because *ella es muy fuerte,*
si es mi mami.
Muy fuerte de caracter.
In a way that I never could be . . .
But perhaps I am.

THE AFTER-INTERVIEW

Sarah Carney

In my work on girls' bodies and the ways white adolescent girls (figure skaters) talk about their physicalness and body experiences within the boundaries of sport, I was determined to attempt to ask questions in such a way as to allow for a discussion of both positive experiences as well as negative ones. The girls I interviewed seemed unable, however, to conceive of alternative discourses for their bodies and physical experience. They provided to me, as if by rote at times, the popular views of the culture; namely, that white girls worry about their weight and that the sport of figure skating contains within it some of the most weight and physical appearance–obsessed adolescents on the planet. I tried to reassure them, and explained that I was just as interested in what they *liked* about their bodies as much as what they did not; however, the girls I was interviewing gave, for the most part, short clear answers about what they had eaten the day of the interview, how they felt about their size, and how much they wished to be smaller, thinner, prettier, and so forth.

Their silence may be understandable; girls' bodies have been under scrutiny for decades. Much of the language used to describe girls' bodies springs primarily from discourses of pathology or deficit. Within the field of psychology, and indeed, within popular culture, girls' bodies (and, in particular, white girls' bodies) are interesting or worth concern/note as anorexic/bulimic systems (Bordo, 1993), as prematurely pregnant, as premature or sexualized children (Walkerdine, 1997), as carriers of the scars of incest and child abuse (Bass & Davis, 1988), and most recently as self-mutilating (Egan, 1997). These languages of pathology have infiltrated our society and, as a result, we—and young women certainly—have at our disposal a limited language from which to describe girls' physicalness as well as physical experience.

"Oh . . . you want to know if I eat well?" asked one skater at the beginning of the interview. "What are you going to ask me about . . . eating disorders?" began another. My study, furthermore and unbeknownst to me, became tagged as "her project on anorexia" by the parents and staff at the rink . . . the same parents who later wanted to know if their daughters had admitted to disordered eating or body image "problems" during the interviews. "Is she on the borderline?" one parent asked me for a diagnosis.

Clearly, given these data from my initial interviews, adolescent girls were extremely adept at using a pathology discourse to describe their bodies; they were equally proficient at using that language to describe the bodies of others. (At one rink where I coach, fellow skaters are either described as "sticks" or "blobs" by other skaters.) However, I was finding at the same time that peeking out behind the sometimes overwhelmingly negative, often mean, disordered, diseased discourses, these girls *were* struggling with conceptualizing their bodies in terms other than issues of body weight or appearance, and their visible efforts in describing bodily possibilities or physical triumphs flagged, for me, the lack of a cultural language for imagining girls' bodies in different or more generous ways. In acknowledging the influence of dominant cultural discourses on the ways in which people make sense of their lives, we as researchers have been forced to confront questions about the data we collect by qualitative interview methods. Perhaps these questions become most salient for those of us who wish to become researchers who seek to uncover previously untold, suppressed, or ignored realities. Many of us who are interested in questioning/overturning dominant cultural ideologies have had the experience of collecting data from participants whom we know are victimized by these discourses of domination, only to find that they use the same languages, the same constructions, and follow the same strict and limited guidelines for "normalcy" that have oppressed them. We expect and search for languages of resistance . . . we find languages of what looks like reproduction.

I began noticing that the girls I had already interviewed were interested in continuing our conversations after the interview was over . . . they began sidling back up to me to tell me more. Hours, days, even weeks could go by between the actual interview event and when they approached me again, but slowly, haltingly, my participants began speaking in a language that was not the reproductive, clear, concise version of reality they had given me before. "Remember when you asked me . . ." one girl started out. And with such beginnings what would come out of these girls' mouths, those same girls who had listed their caloric intakes so exactingly, would be amazing, beautiful, gentle, forgiving, funny, playful, creative, and surprising thoughts about the use of their bodies, their participation in physical activity, and the joy they took in expressing themselves and their bodies through the sport of figure skating. These were not fluent, seamless stories—they were full of fits and starts . . . pauses . . . hesitations . . . and nervous laughter. They were told on the run—in parking lots, while holding doors, between skating sessions, during lessons, in cars, or as we said good-bye. Regardless of where these stories were told however, it seemed clear to me that they were data . . . at least they were just as much legitimate data as the interviews I had so painstakingly collected.

At one point I began bringing my notebook out on the ice while I taught my lessons so that I could record the things they were saying when there was no formal interview or no tape recorder running. Its now nearly filled contents have become invaluable. Between lessons, on the stairs, in bathrooms, and in snack bars, I scribbled in my notebook frantically. Though no tape recorder was running, I was determined to honor the complex message offered by my participants who were so willing to engage themselves and think deeply about the questions I had asked.

For instance, Melanie, a skater who was so poignantly aware of being "too tall" or "too big" to be successful, came up to me after a session not long after I interviewed her. In my notes I recorded her words as best I could: "Did you see me? Did you see my lutz? It was so BIG! It was HUGE! I couldn't believe it . . . I couldn't believe I could jump so high . . . it was so big." Once feared, "big" has become glorious. Another skater, Sandy, says: "I think a good adjective for skating is thrilling . . . because you get to . . . you get to flow along with the wind in your face . . . and you get to be up in the air . . . and you get to be spinning around . . . and . . . I don't know." Ellen, 13, explains: "On the ice no one is there . . . it's so quiet you know . . . quiet and peaceful. Like I'm resting . . . just gliding around." Later, during her skating lesson she turns to me and says: [laughing] "I feel like a fish." [I say something that resembles encouragement to go on and elaborate.] "Like I'm slipping and sliding between people . . . in and out . . . I'm quick and fast and [laughing] this sounds dumb." [No, I say.] "You can't catch me, I'm slippery and cold. . . . " She can't finish because she starts laughing and shrugs her shoulders. Among and between the often contradictory languages of pathology and deprivation currently dominating the field of psychology as well as the media, these girls were struggling to speak in ways that celebrate their physicalness—ways that embrace their strength, their playfulness, their power, their beauty, their grace, and their pleasure in what their bodies can do.

If we listen only to the spoken, first-interview–framed (legitimated) narratives of our participants—if we create parameters for data collection that are narrow and fixed—we run the risk of bringing back only sad stories of reproduction . . . mere confirmations and demonstrations of the incredible power of oppression. The culturally dominant languages are that strong and difficult to overcome, and for many of us, our research participants are or will be reluctant narrators of stories that run counter to dominant cultural languages and conceptions. If, however, we listen to the whispers, to the conversations on the stairs, to the sometimes stumbling attempts to re-say what was said before, we may find that interviews are limited only by the parameters/rules we place on them. The "after-interview," or the "after-interview method," or the "off-handed conversational data collection method," may be one way to complicate stories that seem frighteningly reproductive.

FITFUL NARRATIVES: THE TEXTUAL CONSEQUENCES OF ABUSE

Corrine C. Bertram

Feminist and qualitative researchers have argued that researchers should strive to uncover the silences in narratives and give voice to those who have historically been denied their speech through the denial of their experiences. Fine and Weis (1996) have complicated the ease of uncovering these voices in a recent essay. They propose that narratives cannot stand on their own without sufficient analysis because our informants are sometimes less than critical of their circumstances, oftentimes using self-blame to explain the unjust conditions of their lives and struggling against explanations that approach structural causes of injustice. Without adequate context and analysis, these narratives run the risk of reproducing the silences qualitative researchers wish to uncover.

Recently, it has been suggested that the narratives of survivors of sexual abuse/violence be contextualized within psychological memory research and the views being promoted by the Philadelphia-based False Memory Syndrome Foundation. Although this move to contextualize narratives has thus far been directed almost exclusively toward therapeutic practice, it seems unlikely that any researcher or research project that focuses on narratives of violence will be untouched. Popular culture and mainstream audiences will undoubtedly read the narratives we present as researchers through this lens. In an effort to address this questioning of narratives, what do these "new" readings of survivor narratives mean to researchers who aren't engaged in clinical practice with survivors but nonetheless have a political commitment to ending violence and working against it?

Between 1993 and 1995, I was a research assistant on a project that analyzed the narratives of a racially diverse group of poor and working-class young women and men who had come of age during the Reagan-Bush years. One of the things that the diverse group of women we interviewed shared was a history of violence from intimates (Weis, Fine, Proweller, Bertram, & Marusza, 1998). In some ways, I felt a kinship with these women. I, too, had come of age during the late 1970s and 1980s in the (white) working class, although in the rural Midwest, not the urban Northeast. My family had "fallen from grace" (Newman, 1988) during these years, filing bankruptcy, losing our home and anything the bank could sell to pay off the remainder of my family's debts. I felt this class connection, an inheritance of loss (Allison, 1998), but I also felt a kinship that preceded my class consciousness, one of abuse at the hands of family.

I coded most of the interviews for the project in one of the two cities where the interviews took place. The coding of some of the women's narratives was challenging because of the fitful character of some of their stories, particularly surrounding abuse. Although I use the term *narrative*, most of the stories that I am referring to wouldn't qualify as such given the requirements of narrative theory including, but not limited to, a beginning, middle, and end, a turning point (Bruner, 1990), agency of the narrator (Genovese, 1993), redemption (Carney, 1997), and an overarching coherence and consistency. Rather, these narratives are full of gasps, stutters, lapses, uncertainty. Their accounts of the abuse in their homes or the homes of their family members are marked with silences, silences that they remark upon during their narratives, analyzing their own fitful speech. In one interview a woman "forgot" to mention that her boyfriend and the father of her three children set fire to her apartment with her and her children inside. When asked if she had ever experienced violence, another woman responded with a definitive, "No." But on the previous page of the transcript, I read about how her mother beat her. Still another woman described running from her home when she was very young. There was also the time her younger brother died when a stove fell on top of him. But she didn't remember when this happened or how the stove came to rest on his body. The interview sections on violence are marked by phrases like, "from what I remember," "you never forget," "my memory is kind of foggy," "I remember bits and pieces."

What does the current debate over memory and abuse offer either these women or the scholars that wish to analyze their narratives? Unfortunately and fortunately, these women's narratives have not been included in the current memory/abuse debate. Unfortunately, few question the presence of abuse in the lives of poor and working-class urban women. In fact, reading the recovered memory literature, one would assume that the only women who tell stories of abuse are white, middle-class, and in therapy. Many presume that women who live in urban areas suffer violence and that violence is inevitable in their lives. Their narratives tend to generate complacency rather than outrage, or a move to theorizing repressive mechanisms, or an interruption of the memory encoding process. And while the feminist "speak-out" movement and some talk shows have given women a space to speak, that space is many times confessional or simply constrained (Foucault, 1976/1990; Alcoff & Gray, 1993). What can and cannot be said is so constrained that women who tell stories about more than one occurrence of abuse begin to look like victim personalities, crazy, having an axe to grind, or all three.

For the women we interviewed, poor and working-class, African American, Latino, and white, abuse is one of a constellation of unjust circumstances in their lives. This constellation of violence includes drug abuse and alcoholism, state violence in the form of welfare reform and police brutality, domestic verbal, physical, and sexual violence that they experience themselves or witness from siblings, parents, babysitters, and so forth. Often this violence is gendered, with parents inflicting different punishments for girls than for boys, boyfriends beating girlfriends, police ignoring domestic violence. It is not an interruption of an otherwise uninterrupted life; rather, their lives are marked by disruption, where injustice is par for the course. Within this matrix of discrimination and violence, arson seems less than remarkable.

At present I think feminist psychologists and qualitative researchers have yet to clearly delineate our dual commitments to poststructural narrative theory and the use of our research within public policy centers and legal institutions. On the one hand, we have taken the capital "T" from truth and written of the multiple tellings and constructions of narratives. We have used standpoint theory to define who it is that has the most intimate knowledge of the power structure. On the other hand, we have a commitment to social change within institutions that do not recognize postmodern constructions of the self, let alone multiple readings of the past. Courtrooms and Congress are still capitalizing "Truth."

CONCLUDING REMARKS

We have compiled this collection with the hope that it inspires, in the next generation of researchers, responsible, thoughtful activist research. Our intent is to render public those research quandries and dilemmas that typically remain private, not even articulated in a footnote. As you move into conducting social research, we recommend that you surround yourselves with friends, colleagues, and a community of informants who can help with the crucial decisions you will have to make. Research is not a one (wo)man show. The stories in this text will be joined by your own stories, as we craft a social science that enjoys what Sandra Harding (1991) calls "strong objectivity" and creates what Maxine Greene (1995) calls "a wide awakeness." As you enter the spaces for your work, you will now carry the voices of many graduate students who came before you. And you, too, will confront your own speed bumps, always rewriting the history of social research.

NOTES

CHAPTER 1

1. Data presented in this chapter are drawn from Jersey City. We do, though, speak to the two-city sample since data drawn from both cities are, by and large, remarkably similar by gender, race, and ethnicity.

2. The Latinos in Jersey City author a critique of the police far more expansive than Latinos offered in Buffalo. We explain this discrepancy based on both the physical proximity of Jersey City to New York, where discourses of police harassment and abuse are rampant, and on the long, painful history of corruption in the Jersey City public sector. With respect to City Hall, the schools, and the police and fire departments, Jersey City has had a long history of patronage and favoritism—"cleaned up," in part, only recently. And yet on the ground, community-based suspicion of the schools, the mayor's office, and the police and fire departments remains widespread, particularly in communities of color.

CHAPTER 3

1. Legal scholar Patricia Williams (1997) tells a story of her preschool-age son who was seemingly unable to identify the color of an object. Asked what color the grass was, for example, he would respond, "I don't know" or "It makes no difference." Eventually, Williams discovered that, as she writes,

> The well-meaning teachers at his predominantly white school had valiantly and repeatedly assured their charges that color makes no difference. . . . Yet upon further investigation, the very reason that the teachers had felt it necessary to impart this lesson in the first place was that it did matter, and in predictably cruel ways: some of the children had been fighting about whether black people could play "good guys." (p. 3)

CHAPTER 4

1. I have placed "East Village" in quotes out of respect for the fact that I discovered while I was doing my research, that this name for the neighborhood is

seen as one that was forced onto the people living in the area. The squatters that I was interested in were living in various abandoned buildings in Alphabet City, a section of the lower East Side which is now slowly becoming part of the "East Village" due to the process of gentrification.

2. One could argue here, that perhaps this characterization is correct. These are youth living in a somewhat risky environment. Yet how the committee's concern for these youth gets translated is in question.

3. I must thank Maxine Wolfe, an accomplished activist researcher and tremendous scholar; Rachael Pfeffer (1997), a Ph.D. who created a participatory action dissertation, with and for young women on the streets and in squats; and, of course, my adviser, Michelle Fine who believed in me and offered me much support during this difficult time and beyond.

4. As a colleague (Richard Barry, personal communication, 1997) pointed out, we must always be attentive to the errors which may be present in the tapes we send out to "professional" transcribers. Perception can be clouded by one's ideological bias and can lead to missing and transformed words.

REFERENCES

Alcoff, A., & Gray, L. (1993). Survivor discourse: Transgression or recuperation? *Signs, 18,* 260–290.

Allison, D. (1998). *Cavedweller.* New York: Dutton.

Allport, G. W. (1942). *The use of personal documents in psychological science.* New York: Social Science Research Council.

Anderson, E. (1990). *Streetwise: Race, class, and change in an urban community.* Chicago: University of Chicago Press.

Anzaldua, G. (1981). Speaking in tongues: A letter to third world women writers. In C. Moraga & G. Anzaldua (Eds.), *This bridge called my back: Writings by radical women of color* (pp. 165–173). New York: Kitchen Table Press.

Apfelbaum, E. (1979). Relations of dominating and movement for liberation: An analysis of power between groups. In W. G. Austin & S. Worchel (Eds.), *The social psychology of intergroup relations* (pp. 188–204). Belmont, CA: Wadsworth.

Attar, B. K., Guerra, N. G., & Tolan, P. H. (1994). Neighborhood disadvantages, stressful life events, and adjustment in urban elementary-school children. *Journal of Clinical Child Psychology, 23,* 391–400.

Austin, R. (1992). "The black community," its lawbreakers, and a politics of identification. *Southern California Law Review, 65,* 1769–1817.

Ayala, J., Bertram, C., Carney, S., Centrie, C., Cumiskey, K., Fine, M., Foster, K., Galleta, A., Lombardo, S., Massey, S., McFarlane, T., Christmas, A., Roberts, R., Tocke, K., Valentin, J., Weis, L., & Wesseen, S. (1998). *Speed bumps: Reflections on the politics and methods of qualitative work.* Occasional Paper, Graduate School of Education, State University of New York at Buffalo.

Bandura, A. (1977). *Social learning theory.* Englewood Cliffs, NJ: Prentice-Hall.

Barrett, N. (1994). *The playgroup: Three women contend with the myths of motherhood.* New York: Simon & Schuster.

Bass, E., & Davis, L. (1988). *The courage to heal: A guide for women survivors of sexual abuse.* New York: Harper & Row.

Behar, R. (1993). *Translated woman: Crossing the border with Esperanza's story.* Boston: Beacon Press.

Bell, D. (1989). *And we are not saved: The elusive quest for racial justice.* New York: Basic Books.

Bhavnani, K. K. (1993). Tracing the contours: Feminist research and feminist objectivity. *Women's Studies International Forum, 16,* 95–104.

Billig, M. (1994). Repopulating the depopulated pages of social psychology. *Theory and Psychology, 4*, 307–335.

Billig, M. (1995). *Banal nationalism*. London: Sage.

Bogdan, R., & Biklen, S. (1982). *Qualitative research for education*. Boston: Allyn and Bacon.

Bogdan, R., & Taylor, S. (1975). *Introduction to qualitative methods: A phenomenological approach to the social sciences*. New York: John Wiley and Sons.

Bordo, S. (1993). *Unbearable weight: Feminism, Western culture, and the body*. Berkeley: University of California Press.

Borland, K. (1991). "That's not what I said": Interpretive conflict in moral narrative research. In S. B. Gluck & D. Patai (Eds.), *Women's words: The feminist practice of oral history* (pp. 63–76). New York: Routledge.

Bourgois, P. (1995). *In search of respect: Selling crack in el barrio*. Cambridge, UK: Cambridge University Press.

Bruner, J. (1990). *Acts of meaning*. Cambridge, MA: Harvard University Press.

Brydon-Miller, M. (1998). Participatory action research: Psychology and change. *Journal of Social Issues, 53*, 657–666.

Carney, S. (1997). *The construction of counter-story narratives: A negotiation of resistance and reconciliation*. Master's thesis proposal, City University of New York, Graduate School and University Center, New York.

Chataway, C. J. (1998). An examination of the constraints on mutual inquiry in a participatory action research project. *Journal of Social Issues, 53*, 747–765.

Clifford, J. (1986). On ethnographic allegory. In J. Clifford & G. E. Marcus (Eds.), *Writing culture: The poetics and politics of ethnography* (pp. 98–121). Berkeley: University of California Press.

Clough, P. T. (1992). *The end(s) of ethnography: From realism to social criticism*. Newbury Park, CA: Sage.

Crenshaw, K. (1989). Demarginalizing the intersection of race and sex: A black feminist critique of anti-discrimination doctrine, feminist theory, and anti-racist politics. *University of Chicago Legal Forum*, 139–167.

Cross, W. E., Jr. (1991). *Shades of black: Diversity in African-American identity*. Philadelphia: Temple University Press.

Currie, E. (1993, November). *Missing pieces: Notes on crime, poverty, and social policy*. Paper prepared for the Social Science Research Council, Committee for Research on the Urban Underclass, Policy Conference on Persistent Urban Poverty, Washington, DC.

Denzin, N., & Lincoln, Y. (Eds.). (1994). *Handbook of qualitative research*. Thousand Oaks, CA: Sage.

Dyson, M. E. (1993). *Reflecting black: African-American cultural criticism*. Minneapolis: University of Minnesota Press.

Edin, K., & Lein, L. (1997). *Making ends meet: How single mothers survive welfare and low-wage work*. New York: Russell Sage Foundation.

Egan, J. (1997, July 27). The thin red line. *New York Times Magazine*, 21–25, 40, 43–44, 48.

Espin, O. (1994). Traumatic historic events and adolescent psychosocial development: Letters from V. In C. E. Franz & A. J. Stewart (Eds.), *Women creating lives: Identities, resilience, and resistance* (pp. 187–198). Boulder, CO: Westview Press.

Fagan, J., Conley, D., Debro, J., Curtis, R., Hamid, A., Moore, J., Padilla, F., Quicker, J., Taylor, C., & Vigil, J. D. (1993, November). *Crime, drugs, and neighborhood change: The effects of deindustrialization on social control in inner cities.* Paper prepared for the Social Science Research Council, Committee for Research on the Urban Underclass, Policy Conference on Persistent Urban Poverty, Washington, DC.

Fine, M. (1991). *Framing dropouts: Notes on the politics of an urban public high school.* Albany: State University of New York Press.

Fine, M. (Ed.). (1992). *Disruptive voices: The possibilities of feminist research.* Ann Arbor: University of Michigan Press.

Fine, M. (1993). [Ap]parent involvement: Reflections on parents, power, and urban public schools. *Teachers College Record, 94,* 682–710.

Fine, M. (1994). Working the hyphens: Reinventing self and other in qualitative research. In N. R. Denzin & Y. S. Lincoln (Eds.), *Handbook of qualitative research* (pp. 70–82). Thousand Oaks, CA: Sage.

Fine, M., & Cook, D. (1991). *Evaluation reports "with and for parents."* Washington, DC: National Committee of Citizens for Education.

Fine, M., & Gordon, S. M. (1992). Feminist transformations of/despite psychology. In M. Fine (Ed.), *Disruptive voices: The possibilities of feminist research* (pp. 1–25). Ann Arbor: University of Michigan Press.

Fine, M., Weis, L., Powell, L., & Wong, M. (1997). *Off white: Readings on race, power, and society.* New York: Routledge.

Fine, M., & Vanderslice, V. (1992). Qualitative activist research: Reflections in methods and politics. In F. B. Bryant, J. Edwards, R. S. Tindale, E. J. Posavac, L. Heath, E. Henderson, & Y. Suarez-Balcazar (Eds.), *Methodological issues in applied social psychology* [*Vol. 2 of Social psychological applications to social issues*] (pp. 199–218). New York: Plenum.

Fine, M., & Weis, L. (1996). Writing the "wrongs" of fieldwork: Confronting our own research/writing dilemmas in urban ethnographies. *Qualitative Inquiry, 2,* 251–274.

Fine, M., & Weis, L. (1998). *The unknown city: The lives of poor and working class young adults.* Boston: Beacon.

Flores, W. V., & Benmayor, R. (1997). *Latino cultural citizenship: Claiming identity, space and rights.* Boston: Beacon.

Fordham, S. (1997). Those loud black girls: (Black) women, silence, and gender "passing" in the academy. In M. Seller & L. Weis (Eds.), *Beyond black and white: New faces and voices in U.S. schools.* Albany: State University of New York Press.

Foucault, M. (1990). *The history of sexuality: Vol. 1. An introduction* (R. Hurley, Trans.). New York: Vintage. (Original work published 1976)

Genovese, T. (1993). *Disclosing abuse: Silence and telling.* Paper presented at the 14th Ethnography in Education Conference, University of Pennsylvania, Philadelphia.

Giroux, H. (1983). Theories of reproduction and resistance in the new sociology of education: A critical analysis. *Harvard Educational Review, 43*, 41–77.

Gates, H. L., Jr. (Ed.). (1986). *"Race," writing, and difference.* Chicago: University of Chicago Press.

Gittell, M. J. (1990). Women on foundation boards: The illusion of change. *Women and Foundations/Corporate Philanthropy, 1*, 1–2.

Gittell, M. J. (1994). School reform in New York and Chicago: Revisiting the ecology of local games. *Urban Affairs Quarterly, 30*, 136–151.

Goetz, J. P., & LeCompte, M. (1984). *Ethnography and qualitative design in educational research.* Orlando, FL: Academic Press.

Greene, M. (1995). *Releasing the imagination.* San Francisco: Jossey-Bass.

Hall, S. (1981). Moving right. *The Socialist Review, 55*, 113–137.

Hall, S. (1997). Subjects in history: Making diasporic identities. In W. Lubiano (Ed.), *The house that race built: Black Americans, U.S. terrain* (pp. 289–299). New York: Pantheon.

Haraway, D. (1991). *Simians, cyborgs, and women: The reinvention of nature.* New York: Routledge.

Harding, S. (1991). *Whose science, whose knowledge?* Ithaca, NY: Cornell University Press.

Hidalgo, N. (1998). Toward a definition of a Latino family research paradigm. *Qualitative Studies in Education, 11*, 103–120.

hooks, b. (1992). Representations of whiteness in the black imagination. In *Black looks: Radical representation.* Boston: South End Press.

Hsieh, C. C., & Pugh, M. D. (1993). Poverty, income, inequality, and violent crime: A meta-analysis of recent aggregate data studies. *Criminal Justice Review, 18*, 182–202.

Hurtado, A., & Stewart, A. J. (1997). Through the looking glass: Implications of studying whiteness for feminist methods. In M. Fine, L. Weis, L. C. Powell, & L. M. Wong (Eds.), *Off white: Readings on race, power, and society* (pp. 297–311). New York: Routledge.

Katz, M. (1995). *Improving poor people.* Princeton, NJ: Princeton University Press.

Kelly, R. D. G. (1997). *Yo' mama's disfunktional! Fighting the culture wars in urban black America.* Boston: Beacon Press.

Kidder, L., & Fine, M. (1997). Qualitative inquiry in psychology: A radical tradition. In D. Fox & I. Prilleltensky (Eds.), *Critical psychology: An introduction* (pp. 34–50). Thousand Oaks, CA: Sage.

Kincheloe, J. L., & McLaren, P. L. (1994). Rethinking critical theory and qualitative research. In N. K. Denzin & Y. S. Lincoln (Eds.), *Handbook of qualitative research* (pp. 138–157). Thousand Oaks, CA: Sage.

Ladner, J. A. (1971). *Tomorrow's tomorrow: The black woman.* Garden City, NY: Doubleday.

Lal, J. (1996). Situating locations. In D. L. Wolf (Ed.), *Feminist dilemmas in fieldwork* (pp. 185–214). Boulder, CO: Westview Press.

Lather, P. (1986). Research as practice. *Harvard Educational Review, 56*(3), 257–277.

Lather, P. (1991). *Getting smart: Feminist research pedagogy within the postmodern.* New York: Routledge.

Lawrence, C. R., III. (1995). The word and the river: Pedagogy as scholarship as struggle. In K. Crenshaw, N. Gotanda, G. Peller, & K. Thomas (Eds.), *Critical race theory: The key writings that formed the movement* (pp. 336–351). New York: New Press.

LeCompte, M., & Schensul, J. J. (1999). *Designing and conducting ethnographic work* (Book One). Walnut Creek, CA: Altamira Press.

Lewis, M. G. (1993). *Without a word: Teaching beyond women's silence.* New York: Routledge.

Lykes, M. B. (1989). Dialogue with Guatemalan Indian women: Critical perspectives on constructing collaborative research. In R. K. Unger (Ed.), *Representations: Social constructions of gender* (pp. 167–185). Amityville, NY: Baywood Publishing.

Lykes, M. B. (1994). Speaking against the silence: One Maya woman's exile and return. In C. E. Franz & A. J. Stewart (Eds.), *Women creating lives: Identities, resilience, and resistance* (pp. 97–114). Boulder, CO: Westview Press.

Lykes, M. B. (1998). Activist participatory research among the Maya of Guatemala: Constructing meanings from situated knowledge. *Journal of Social Issues, 53,* 725–746.

Lykes, B., Banuazizi, A., Liem, R., & Morris, M. (Eds.). (1996). *Myths about the powerless: Contesting social inequalities.* Philadelphia, PA: Temple University Press.

MacLeod, J. (1995). *Ain't no making it: Aspirations and attainment in a low-income neighborhood* (2nd ed.). Boulder, CO: Westview.

Madigan, R., Johnson, S., & Linton, P. (1995). The language of psychology: APA style as epistemology. *American Psychologist, 50,* 428–436.

Mann, P. (1994). *Micro-politics: Agency in a postfeminist era.* Minneapolis: University of Minnesota Press.

Matsuda, M. (1995). Looking to the bottom: Critical legal studies and reparations. In K. Crenshaw, N. Gotanda, G. Peller, & K. Thomas (Eds.), *Critical race theory: The key writings that formed the movement* (pp. 63–79). New York: New Press.

Maxwell, J. A. (1992). Understanding and validity in qualitative research. *Harvard Educational Review, 62,* 279–301.

McCarthy, C., Rodriguez, A., Meecham, S., David, S., Wilson-Brown, C., Godina, H., Supryia, K., & Buendia, E. (1997). Race, suburban resentment, and the representation of the inner city in contemporary film and television. In M. Fine,

L. Weis, L. Powell, & M. Wong (Eds.), *Off white: Readings on race, power, and society* (pp. 229–241). New York: Routledge.

Morawski, J. G., & Bayer, B. M. (1995). Stirring trouble and making theory. In H. Landrine (Ed.), *Bringing cultural diversity to feminist psychology: Theory, research, and practice* (pp. 113–137). Washington, D.C.: American Psychological Association.

Morgan, D. (1988). *Focus groups as qualitative research.* Newburg, CA: Sage.

Mullings, L. (1984). Minority women, work and health. In W. Chavkin (Ed.), *Double exposure: Women's health hazards on the job and at home* (pp. 84–106). New York: Monthly Review Press.

Nagata, D. (1990). The Japanese-American internment: Perceptions of moral community, fairness, and redress. *Journal of Social Issues, 46,* 133–146.

Newman, K. S. (1988). *Falling from grace: The experience of downward mobility in the American middle class.* New York: Vintage.

Okely, J. (1992). Anthropology and autobiography: Participatory experience and embodied knowledge. In J. Okely & H. Callaway (Eds.), *Anthropology and autobiography* (pp. 1–49). London: Routledge.

Oliver, M., & Shapiro, T. (1995). *Black wealth/white wealth: A new perspective on racial inequality.* New York: Routledge.

Omi, M., & Winant, H. (1986). *Racial formations in the United States.* New York: Routledge.

Opotow, S. (1990). Moral exclusion and injustice: An introduction. *Journal of Social Issues, 46,* 1–20.

Pfeffer, R. (1997). *Surviving the streets: Girls living on their own.* New York: Garland.

Piven, F. F., Block, F., Cloward, R. A., & Ehrenreich, B. (1987). *The mean season.* New York: Pantheon.

Piven, F. F., & Cloward, R. A. (1971). *Regulating the poor: The functions of public welfare.* New York: Pantheon.

Piven, F. F., & Cloward, R. A. (1977). *Poor people's movements: Why they succeed, how they fail.* New York: Pantheon.

Powell, L. (1994). Interpreting social defenses: Family group in an urban setting. In M. Fine (Ed.), *Chartering urban school reform: Reflections on public high schools in the midst of change* (pp. 112–121). New York: Teachers College Press.

Richardson, L. (1994). Writing: A method of inquiry. In N. K. Denzin & Y. S. Lincoln (Eds.), *Handbook of qualitative research* (pp. 516–529). Thousand Oaks, CA: Sage.

Richardson, L. (1995). Writing-stories: Co-authoring "The Sea Monster," a writing-story. *Qualitative Inquiry, 1,* 189–203.

Roman, L. (1993). Double exposure: The politics of feminist materialist ethnography. *Educational Theory, 43,* 279–308.

Roman, L. (1996). Spectacle in the dark: Youth as transgression, display, and regression. *Educational Theory, 46,* 1–22.

Roman, L. (1997). Denying (white) racial privilege: Redemption discourses and the uses of fantasy. In M. Fine, L. Weis, L. C. Powell, & L. M. Wong (Eds.), *Off white: Readings on race, power, and society* (pp. 270–282). New York: Routledge.

Rosaldo, R. (1989). *Culture and truth: The remaking of social analysis.* Boston: Beacon Press.

Saegert, S. (1997, May). *Schools and the ecology of gender.* Paper presented at the Schools and the Urban Environment Conference, National Taiwan University, Taipei, Taiwan.

Schwab-Stone, M. E., Ayers, T. S., Kasprow, W., & Voyce, C. (1995). No safe haven: A study of violence exposure in urban communities. *Journal of the American Academy of Child and Adolescent Psychiatry, 34,* 1343–1352.

Scott, D. M. (1997). *Contempt and pity: Social policy and the image of the damaged Black psyche 1880–1996.* Chapel Hill: University of North Carolina Press.

Scott, J. W. (1992). Experience. In J. Butler & J. W. Scott (Eds.), *Feminists theorize the political* (pp. 22–40). New York: Routledge.

Sedgwick, E. (1990). *Epistemology of the closet.* Berkeley: University of California Press.

Stacey, J. (1991). Can there be a feminist ethnography? In S. B. Gluck & D. Patai (Eds.), *Women's words: The feminist practice of oral history* (pp. 111–119). New York: Routledge.

Stewart, A. J., Franz, C., & Layton, L. (1988). The changing self: Using personal documents to study lives. *Journal of Personality, 56,* 41–74.

Sullivan, M. L. (1989). *"Getting paid": Youth crime and work in the inner city.* Ithaca, NY: Cornell University Press.

Suls, J. M., & Rosnow, R. L. (1988). Concerns about artifacts in psychological experiments. In J. G. Morawski (Ed.), *The rise of experimentation in American psychology* (pp. 163–187). New Haven, CT: Yale University Press.

Tolman, D. (1994). Daring to desire: Culture and the body of adolescent girls. In J. M. Irvine (Ed.), *Sex culture and constructing adolescent identities* (pp. 250–284). Philadelphia, PA: Temple University Press.

Walkerdine, V. (1997). *Daddy's girl: Young girls and popular culture.* Cambridge, MA: Harvard University Press.

Watters, E. (1993, January/February). Doors of memory. *Mother Jones,* 24–29, 76–77.

Weis, L. (1985). *Between two worlds: Black students in an urban community college.* New York: Routledge.

Weis, L. (1990). *Working class without work: High school students in a de-industrializing economy.* New York: Routledge.

Weis, L., & Fine, M. (Eds.). (1993). *Beyond silenced voices: Class, race, and gender in United States schools.* Albany: State University of New York Press.

Weis, L., & Fine, M. (1996). Narrating the 1980s and 1990s: Voices of poor and working class white and African American men. *Anthropology and Education, 27,* 1–24.

Weis, L., & Fine, M. (Eds.). (2000). *Construction sites: Excavating race, class, and gender among urban youth*. New York: Teachers College Press.

Weis, L., Fine, M., Proweller, A., Bertram, C., & Marusza, J. (1998). "I've slept in clothes long enough": Excavating the sounds of domestic violence among urban women in the white working class. *The Urban Review, 30*, 1–27.

Weis, L., Marusza, J., & Fine, M. (1998). Out of the cupboard: Kids, domestic violence and schools. *British Journal of Sociology of Education, 19*, 53–73.

Weis, L., Proweller, A., & Centrie, C. (1997). Re-examining "A moment in history": Loss of privilege inside white working-class masculinity in the 1990's. In M. Fine, L. Weis, L. C. Powell, & L. M. Wong (Eds.), *Off white: Readings on race, power, and society* (pp. 210–226). New York: Routledge.

West, C. (1993). *Race matters*. Boston: Beacon Press.

Williams, P. J. (1997). *Seeing a color-blind future: The paradox of race*. New York: Farrar, Straus & Giroux.

Wilson, W. J. (1987). *The truly disadvantaged: The inner city, the underclass and public policy*. Chicago: University of Chicago Press.

Woolf, V. (1944). *A haunted house and other stories*. New York: Harcourt, Brace & World. (Original work published 1921)

INDEX

ABOUT THE AUTHORS

Lois Weis is Professor of Sociology of Education at the State University of New York at Buffalo. She is the author and/or editor of numerous books and articles on the subject of social class, race, gender, and schooling. Her most recent publications include *The Unknown City: The Lives of Poor and Working Class Young Adults* (with Michelle Fine); *Working Class Without Work: High School Students in a De-Industrializing Economy*; *Beyond Silenced Voices* (with Michelle Fine); *Beyond Black and White* (with Maxine Seller); and *Off White* (with Michelle Fine, Linda Powell, and Mun Wong). She sits on several editorial boards and is a past editor of *Educational Policy*.

Michelle Fine is Professor of Social Psychology at the Graduate Center of the City University of New York. Her numerous articles and books include *The Unknown City* (with Lois Weis); *Framing Dropouts: Notes on the Politics of an Urban Public High School*; and *Becoming Gentlemen: Women, Law School, and Institutional Change* (with Lani Guinier and Jane Balin).